"The aspect of the venerable mansion has always affected me like a human countenance, bearing the traces not merely of outward storm and sunshine, but expressive also of the long lapse of mortal life and accompanying vicissitudes that have passed within."

Nathaniel Hawthorne, *The House of the Seven Gables*, 1851

INDOWS *on the* PAST

LANDER WITH DIANE L. VIERA

OR THE PRESERVATION OF NEW ENGLAND ANTIQUITIES

D BY WENDELL GARRETT

FOUR CENTURIES OF NEW ENGLAND HO[M]

COLOR PHOTOGRAPHS BY DAVID

BULFINCH PRESS/LITTLE, BROWN AND COM[PANY]

BOSTON • NEW YORK • LO[NDON]

Foreword by Wendell Garrett   9

Introduction: Windows on the Past   12

NEW ENGLAND ON THE MIND 18

CULTIVATING EDEN 39

TIME-HONORED HOUSES 59

ROOMS OF THEIR OWN 81

TIES THAT BIND 105

COMFORT AND CONVENIENCE 128

AT THE TABLE 155

REMEMBERING THE PAST 174

Properties of the Society for the Preservation
of New England Antiquities   198

Further Reading   204

Acknowledgments   205

Index   206

FOREWORD

"Our ancestors sought a new continent," said James Russell Lowell in 1866. "What they found was a new condition of mind." The Revolution reversed Americans' loyalty to the king of England with astonishing abruptness. As John Adams put it in 1818, "The radical change in the principles, opinions, sentiments, and affections of the people was the real American Revolution." Yet the rejection of Britain was tempered by ambivalence, and it may be that this selective attitude toward the colonial past helps explain the differences between Americans and the English in general and the uniqueness of American architecture and furniture in particular. The national consciousness that flourished in the republic's early years may be interpreted positively as the expression of a cultural identity distinct from England's or negatively as a deplorable example of cultural insularity.

opposite

Behind Forest Hall, the Barrett House in New Ipswich, New Hampshire, stands a Gothic Revival summer house, built around 1840. Sited on top of a terraced hillside, it overlooks more than seventy-five acres of woods, meadows, and gardens.

"After the first Cares for the Necessaries of Life are over, we shall come to think of the Embellishments," Benjamin Franklin confidently wrote in 1763. "Already some of our young Geniuses begin to lisp Attempts at Painting, Poetry, and Musick." "Embellishments," as Franklin noted, were replacing mere comfort in the homes of the rich; comfort was supplanting privation in the houses of the not-so-rich. Yeoman farmers, urban craftsmen, and merchants were building a prosperous and productive society. In constructing houses, planning gardens, and painting or carving furniture, these accomplished amateurs followed the latest pattern books from England. In all of those books, design was controlled by the same preoccupation with order and proportion that governs much of the painting, literature, and music of the time. By 1750 coastal towns such as Portsmouth, Boston, and Newport were already miniature Londons. A new society, graceful and cultivated and following the model of western European culture, was being firmly established along with the edge of the North American wilderness as the frontier of forests and Indians was pushed westward. Paradoxically, Europe's colonizing of the New World was doomed by its success: America had been peopled by the most enterprising of Europeans who could innovate at will thanks to the country's isolation. In the act of flourishing, the New England colonies were ceasing to be European.

However, even the most ardent of nationalists had to admit that America was too new, too raw, and too poor to be able to train, teach, or afford artists, writers, and craftsmen working in anything like the style achieved in the Old World. The absence of a long cultural tradition, the lack of patronage, the indifference of the new federal government, and the neglect of classical learning relegated America to the backwater of European artistic and literary achievement. The work of the best colonial artists could not compare with the finish and polish of their British contemporaries such as Gainsborough, Reynolds, Zoffany, and Stubbs. Literature, too, despite a solitary oak like Franklin, was still in the sapling stage compared with Richardson, Addison, Steele, Johnson, and Boswell. While small clusters of enthusiasts corresponded with scientists overseas, no American experimenters could claim discoveries on a par with the epoch-making work being done in Europe. Likewise, no colonial student of society produced anything nearly equal to Adam Smith's *Wealth of Nations* or Denis Diderot's *Encyclopédie*. Even in architecture the Old World influence was overwhelming. Still, it is of some significance that in 1756 the lexicographer Samuel Johnson was talking of an American dialect in speech. And the early architecture and furniture illustrated and discussed in this book demonstrate the ways in which Americans' consciousness of themselves was growing and in which the future was more than implicit. The buildings and objects owned by the Society for the Preservation of New England Antiquities (SPNEA) emphasize the divergence of American practice from English models. In these designs we catch the first glimmers of an emerging American style. These New Englanders, urban and rural, even in the diversity of their moods, shared the belief that a new day in human history had dawned.

Walt Whitman once wrote that to understand America one had to appreciate "the pull-down-and-build-over-again spirit" he witnessed in New York City. He was carried away by the restless—and wasteful—national desire to destroy the old and replace it with the new. And it is true: no other nation has so deliberately and repetitively torn down its buildings of architectural importance and monuments of irreplaceable value. It was in the teeth of this sort of avarice and expediency that President Charles W. Eliot of Harvard, with Wendell Phillips, James Russell Lowell, Oliver Wendell Holmes, and others banded together in 1877 to arouse the populace against the wanton destruction of the 1729 Old South Meeting House in Boston—the scene of meetings that fomented the American Revolution. The purchase and preservation of the building in the face of impossible odds was an early source of inspiration to preservationists and antiquarians all over the nation.

A new direction in the preservation of our architectural heritage was heralded by the antiquarian William Sumner Appleton, the founder of SPNEA in 1910, whose stated purpose was

to save for future generations structures of the seventeenth and eighteenth centuries and the early years of the nineteenth, which are architecturally beautiful and unique, or have special historical significance. Such buildings once destroyed can never be replaced.

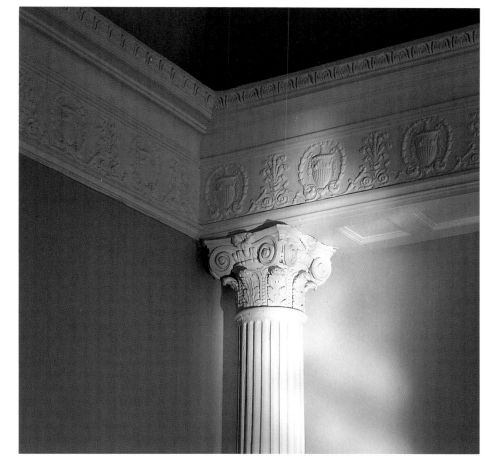

During the intervening ninety years Americans have become convinced that saving old buildings for future generations is a form of progress. SPNEA's diverse, and in many ways unique, buildings and collection vividly reflect the disparate strands of the emerging American culture. There is a functional beauty in these peculiarly American buildings of utility and objects of adornment. Like most men and women, the New Englanders who made and used these things and lived and worked in these structures were caught up in unrelenting and sometimes incomprehensible forces of change. As they moved one foot forward into the future, they left the other firmly planted in the past. Indeed, in their ambivalence, their inconsistency, their capacity for irony, and their expressions of fear and hope, they look singularly familiar to our own age. SPNEA is to be wholeheartedly congratulated for its significant accomplishments and enlightened stewardship in the Northeast over the past nine decades. For "New England is," in the felicitous words of the poet David McCord, "the authorized version of America: her land and people chapter and verse for more than three hundred years."

Wendell Garrett

WINDOWS ON THE PAST

"Built 1737 by Thomas Hancock. Destroyed 1863. The fate of [the John Hancock House] has become a classic in the annals of vandalism. Governor Hancock is said to have intended to bequeath his home to the Commonwealth, but he died without giving effect to this intention by will. In 1859 a strong effort was made to have the Commonwealth purchase the house at a low valuation. This effort failed, and later the heirs offered the house with some of its contents to the city as a free gift, the house to be moved to another site. This plan also failed, and in 1863 the house was destroyed."

William Sumner Appleton,
Bulletin of the Society for the Preservation of New England Antiquities,
May 1910

Forty-seven years after John Hancock's Beacon Street house in Boston was demolished, William Sumner Appleton could write as passionately about the loss as if it had just occurred, denouncing it on the first page of the first issue of the *Bulletin,* the quarterly journal of his newly founded Society for the Preservation of New England Antiquities. As the nineteenth century headed for the twentieth, most historical societies and preservation efforts, lacking the vision or sufficient funding to have an impact throughout the region, attempted only to salvage single buildings. No laws existed to protect any historic sites; acquisition was often the only way to guarantee long-term preservation and sensitive care.

In 1905 a movement began in Boston to save the Paul Revere House, built 1676–82 and the oldest remaining building in the city. The house was saved by Jonathan Phillips Reynolds Jr., a Revere descendant who purchased it and formed the Paul Revere Association to oversee its restoration. Appleton, then thirty-one years old, became the association's secretary. Thus began his formal interest in preservation, which became his life's work.

In 1910, using his own resources and those of a few friends—Charles Bolton, Ernest Gay, Alice Longfellow, and others—Appleton started SPNEA to establish "a large and strong society, which shall cover the whole field and act instantly wherever needed to lead in the preservation of noteworthy buildings and historic sites." Appleton and the other SPNEA founders saw buildings as the framework for creating an understanding of daily life and cultural values of earlier times. The organization moved quickly to purchase several early Massachusetts houses, beginning with the Swett-Ilsley House in Newbury, built about 1670; the Fowler House in Danvers, built in 1809 (no longer owned by SPNEA); and the Cooper-Frost-Austin House in Cambridge, built about 1690. The collection grew rapidly; over the years SPNEA has owned more than one hundred historic properties, some of which it purchased outright and some of which were donated. SPNEA also found time to counsel those who wished to preserve and care for other buildings.

During its first fifty years, SPNEA's aim was to preserve buildings of the seventeenth and eighteenth centuries. Standard practice during this time was to remove later additions and evidence of successive architectural changes (although restoration work was carefully documented through photographs and written field notes). In 1969, however, SPNEA acquired the Codman House in Lincoln, Massachusetts, which had been altered and expanded at least four times since 1740 and contained furnishings, paintings, clothing, photographs, and manuscripts spanning more than

pages 12–13

The handblown glass of a window at the Gilman Garrison House in Exeter, New Hampshire, offers a glimpse of the doorway beyond. The house itself serves as a window into the lives of its varied occupants over three centuries, from its original owner, John Gilman, who lived with the constant threat of Indian attack, to William Perry Dudley, who restored it in the 1950s.

two centuries. That year the organization adopted a policy of keeping buildings and their contents intact, retaining all the evidence of changes, new ideas, and various personalities that had left their imprint through the years, rather than recreating what the buildings may have looked like when first constructed. It was thus among the first preservation groups to eschew "restoration" and to carefully preserve and cherish all the layers of history at its sites. Since 1969 no SPNEA building has been accepted without a full complement of family furnishings and related documentary material, and the organization has made many successful efforts to recover items removed before acquisition.

The evolution of SPNEA and its collection reflects changes in historic preservation techniques and parallels the growth of professional and popular interest in architectural, landscape, and social history. SPNEA's historical focus has also expanded. Appleton apparently never seriously considered acquiring a Victorian building or a more modern one, even though he himself could not resist collecting brand-new objects that he believed were documents of life in his own day—art pottery, household furnishings, clothing, stationery, photographs, and postcards. As late as the mid-1950s his successors at SPNEA discarded some furnishings of the Victorian and later periods. Within fifteen years, however, the pendulum had swung back, and SPNEA acquired and began to preserve both Henry Bowen's 1846 Gothic Revival Roseland Cottage in Woodstock, Connecticut, and Walter and Ise Gropius's 1938 Bauhaus-inspired house in Lincoln, Massachusetts, along with their entire contents.

Today, the SPNEA collection, which the American Association of Museums has called perhaps the country's most significant for the interpretation of New England, encompasses 125 buildings on forty-five historic sites in five New England states: Connecticut, Maine, Massachusetts, New Hampshire, and Rhode Island. These houses and outbuildings are located on slightly more than 1,300 acres of land, which ranges from upland woodlands to coastal salt marshes and shows evidence of prehistoric occupation and agriculture by Native Americans as well as nearly four hundred years of changing historic agricultural and horticultural practices and taste.

above

From the window of the sitting-room chamber (the bedroom above the sitting room) at the Sayward-Wheeler House in York Harbor, Maine, family members have watched boat traffic on the York River for nearly three centuries.

At twenty-five sites the houses are furnished and are regularly open to the public as historic house museums (for a complete listing, see pages 198–203). A meeting-house and nine study houses may be visited by appointment or for special programs. Lacking original furnishings, SPNEA's seventeenth-century study houses make no attempt to re-create crowded, smelly, and dynamic domestic interiors of the time. Instead, they offer an unparalleled opportunity to examine the origins of New England architecture and its old housewright traditions in examples that reflect the local abundance of wood, changes in building technology, regional variations, and the evolution of new architectural forms. Some of its properties have been leased to tenants, and some have been transferred to other owners, usually with the protection of easements ensuring long-term preservation of buildings and significant features.

SPNEA also owns more than 110,000 artifacts closely associated with New England families or artisans, half on view in the historic properties and the rest carefully stored but available for formal exhibition and research. The library now contains more than one million historic images and other primary materials in the form of books, manuscripts, photographs, negatives, postcards, stereo cards, daguerreotypes, architectural drawings, and illustrated ephemera.

Because of its extraordinary size and scope, the SPNEA collection offers far more insight into the history of New England and New Englanders than can be explored in this book, whose focus is the twenty-five furnished SPNEA houses that are open as house museums. The families who built these homes were, for the most part, wealthy and privileged, and the houses express their status. SPNEA properties do not yet include examples of the simplest dwellings or wholly vernacular styles of New England houses or represent every architectural style or geographic region. Still, the diversity of the New England experience is reflected in SPNEA's buildings, furnishings, and landscapes. Beyond a review of architectural styles and building techniques, they provide settings for the intimacies of family life, relating the stories of husbands and wives, boys and girls, clever bachelors and lonely old maids, enslaved Africans, hopeful Irish girls, and eastern European immigrants. They tell us of merchants, lawyers, ministers, farmers, politicians, housewives, teachers, authors, and preservationists as well as the architects, interior designers, carpenters, masons, furniture makers, landscape designers, plumbers, and others employed by the owners. To open the door to one of these houses is to open a door onto their lives, which reflect both their individuality and the commonality of human experience.

opposite

The display of glass in windows was a signature decorating technique of Henry Davis Sleeper at Beauport in Gloucester, Massachusetts. In the Franklin Passage he artfully arranged free-blown and blown-molded pieces.

N EW ENGLAND ON THE MIND

"Nature has been bountiful to our land

and we need but the hand of art, skillfully applied,

to render it more lovely and more fruitful."

Christopher Gore (1758–1827), creator of Gore Place (1806) in Waltham, Massachusetts

pages 18–19

Little's Lane at the Spencer-Peirce-Little Farm in Newbury, Massachusetts.

this page and opposite

The Hamilton House, its gardens, and the adjacent Vaughan Woods on the Salmon Falls River in South Berwick, Maine.

"The cold is merely superficial; it is the summer still at the core, far, far within."

Henry David Thoreau,
journal entry,
January 12, 1855

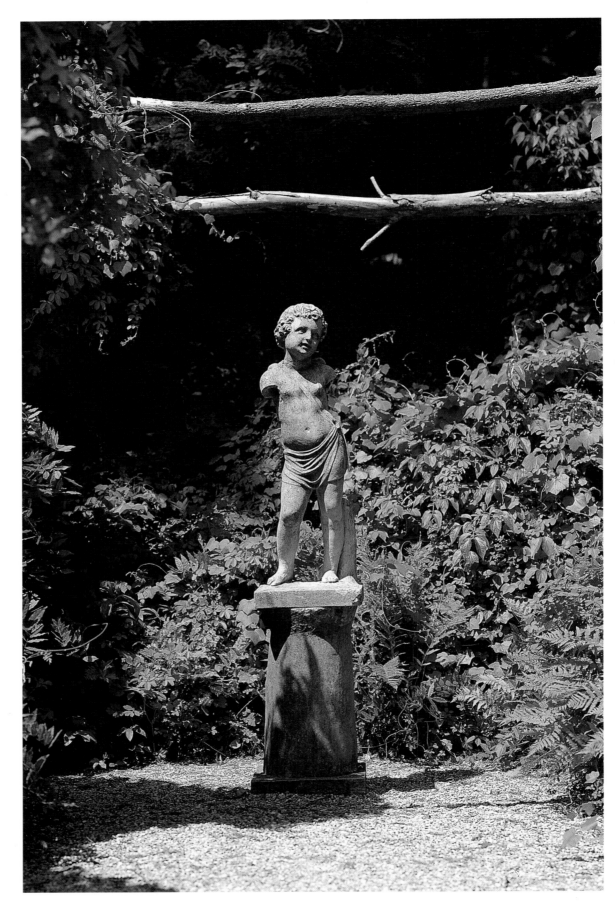

"What I admire and love is the generous and spontaneous [New England] soil which flowers and fruits in all seasons."

Ralph Waldo Emerson, undated journal entry

right

A garden sculpture at the Codman House in Lincoln, Massachusetts.

opposite

Spring beauty at the Governor John Langdon House in Portsmouth, New Hampshire.

"I praise the flower-
barren fields, the
clouds, the tall

Unanswering
branches where
the wind makes
sullen noise.

I praise the fall:
it is the human
season."

Archibald MacLeish,
"Immortal Autumn,"
1930

opposite

A pasture scene at the
Watson Farm in James-
town, Rhode Island.

top left

Tools for productive
agriculture and
ornamental horticul-
ture at the Lyman
Estate in Waltham,
Massachusetts.

top right

The tidal Salmon Falls
River below the Ham-
ilton House in South
Berwick, Maine.

right

Relic stone walls
still bounding a
field at the Codman
House in Lincoln,
Massachusetts.

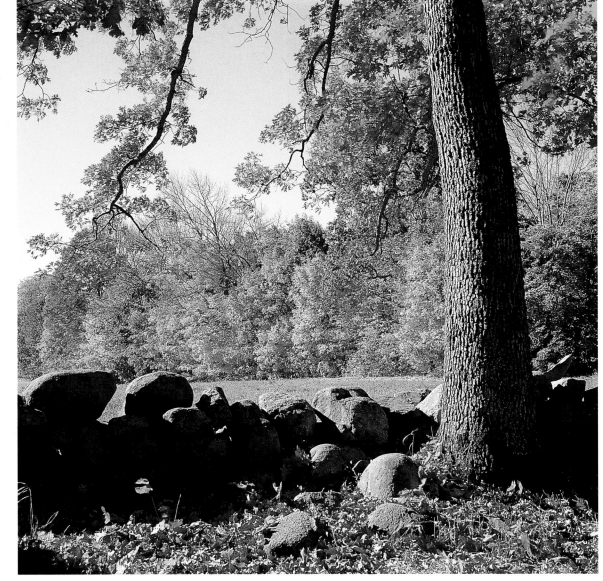

"[T]he lower hall is very fine, with an archway dividing it, and panelings of all sorts, and a great door at each end, through which the lilacs in front and the pensioner plum-trees in the garden are seen exchanging bows and gestures."

Sarah Orne Jewett,
Deephaven, 1877

right

Garlic grown for the Community Supported Agriculture Program at the Casey Farm in Saunderstown, Rhode Island.

opposite

A welcoming door and entry hall at the Barrett House in New Ipswich, New Hampshire.

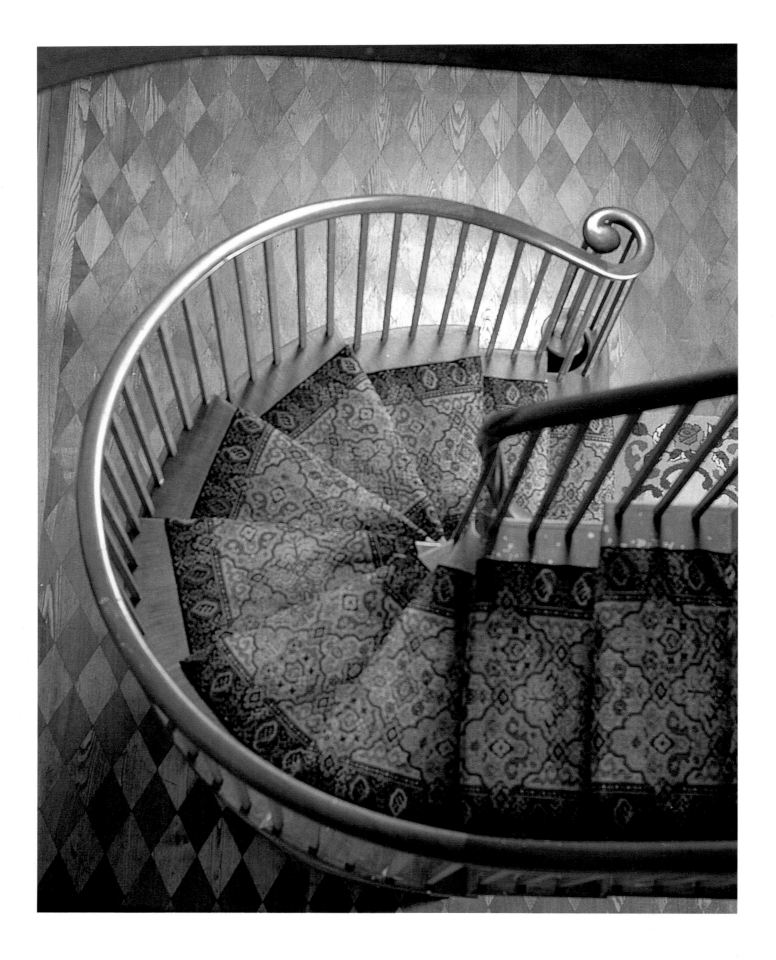

opposite

The stairway at Castle Tucker in Wiscasset, Maine.

right

Stairs to the gallery at the Rocky Hill Meeting House, Ames-bury, Massachusetts.

below

The staircase at the Gropius House in Lincoln, Massachusetts.

"A kind of old Hobgoblin Hall,

Now somewhat fallen to decay,

With weather-stains upon the wall,

And stairways worn, and crazy doors,

And creaking and uneven floors,

And chimneys huge, and tiled and tall."

Henry Wadsworth Longfellow, prelude, "Tales of a Wayside Inn," 1863

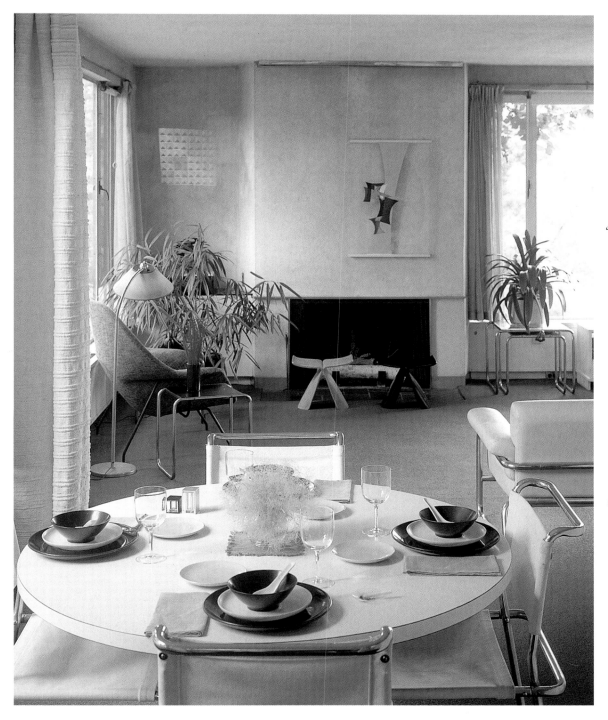

"I love it, I love it;
and who shall dare

To chide me for
loving that old
arm-chair?

I've treasured it
long as a sacred
prize;

I've bedewed
it with tears,
and embalmed it
with sighs;

'Tis bound by
a thousand bands
to my heart;

Not a tie will
break, not a link
will start.

Would ye learn
the spell? a mother
sat there,

And a sacred
thing is that old
arm-chair."

Eliza Cook,
"The Old Arm-Chair,"
Godey's Lady's Book,
March 1855

right

The sinuous curves
of a Grecian sofa
in the parlor of the
Marrett House in
Standish, Maine.

below

Plain paper with
a swag border in
the dining room
of the Otis House
in Boston.

opposite

Scenic wallpaper
in the dining room
of the Barrett House
in New Ipswich,
New Hampshire.

"I was dazzled
by the brilliancy
of the room. . . .
The furniture
was exceedingly
rich. . . . [I]t struck
me that here was
the fulfilment of
every fantasy of
an imagination
revelling in various
methods of costly
self-indulgence
and splendid ease.
Pictures, marbles,
vases,—in brief,
more shapes of
luxury than there
could be any
object in enumer-
ating, except for an
auctioneer's adver-
tisement. . . ."

Nathaniel Hawthorne,
*The Blithedale
Romance*, 1852

above

Plasterwork with
neoclassical details in
the ballroom of the
Lyman Estate in Wal-
tham, Massachusetts.

right

The withdrawing room
of the Otis House,
where a wallpaper
border accentuates
the mantel design.

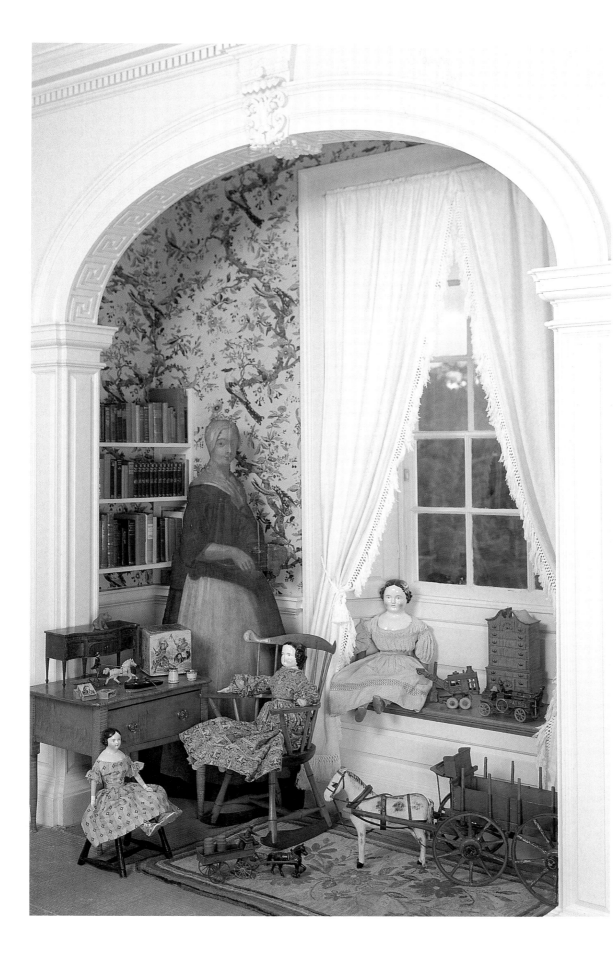

"There was a large cabinet holding all the small curiosities and knick-knacks there seemed to be no other place for,—odd china figures, and cups and vases, unaccountable Chinese carvings and exquisite corals and sea shells, minerals and Swiss wood-work, and articles of *vertu* from the South Seas."

Sarah Orne Jewett,
Deephaven, 1877

opposite

The toolshed's upper story and the barn attic at Castle Tucker in Wiscasset, Maine (top left and right). The Codman House's cellar milk room and attic in Lincoln, Massachusetts (bottom left and right).

left

Dolls and toys at the Hamilton House in South Berwick, Maine.

"Every day a
new picture is
painted and
framed, held up
for half an hour,

in such lights as
the Great Artist
chooses, and then
withdrawn, and
the curtain falls.

And then the sun
goes down, and
long the afterglow
gives light.

And then the
damask curtains
glow along the
western window.

And now the
first star is lit,
and I go home."

Henry David Thoreau,
as quoted in
*Autumn: A New
England Journey* (1988)

above

A sieve, a shovel, and
a coffee grinder in the
buttery at the Coffin
House in Newbury,
Massachusetts.

opposite

Inscribed graffiti
on a gallery pew at
the Rocky Hill Meet-
ing House in Ames-
bury, Massachusetts.

CULTIVATING EDEN

"A village on a hill, white houses facing on a green, tall elms arching overhead, and a white church spire pointing heaven-ward: for many Americans this picture represents stability, tradition, national roots, and a retreat from urban stress."

Alan Emmet, *So Fine a Prospect: Historic New England Gardens*, 1996

left

The exceptionally
large barn at the
Spencer-Peirce-Little
Farm in Newbury,
Massachusetts, built
in the eighteenth
century and still used
today, testifies to the
farm's productivity.

opposite

An aerial view of
Cogswell's Grant in
Essex, Massachusetts,
reveals the farm's
layout: the barn
(left), its equipment
shed and milk room,
and the kitchen
garden beyond; the
house (right) with its
private dooryard;
the farmyard with its
1700s barn; and
pastures and hay-
fields leading to the
salt marsh and the
Essex River.

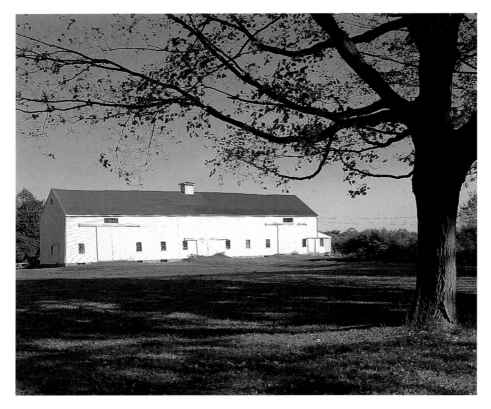

pages 38–39

The quintessential
New England village
of Wiscasset, Maine,
seen from the front
steps of Castle
Tucker, typifies early
New Englanders'
efforts to turn the
land into compact
town centers and tidy
farms. These architec-
tural features are now
considered icons of
the American identity.

Throughout New England's history, the land has been continually reworked and the landscape changed in response to human needs and available resources. The efforts of the first English settlers in the New World in the seventeenth century resulted in an alluring countryside and town centers with characteristic architectural features now considered icons of national identity.

From Maine to Rhode Island, SPNEA's 1,350 acres of New England landscape tell the stories of people who made their living from the land and of others who created intimate gardens as a means of personal expression or who built grand pleasure grounds to showcase their prosperity. Most of these landscapes reveal changing methods of agricultural practices and tastes in garden design as well as natural maturation. In New England today historic landscapes that have remained undivided and have been cared for since the seventeenth century are rare, especially large tracts of farmland. SPNEA, however, preserves the larger part of four such farms: Cogswell's Grant and the Spencer-Peirce-Little Farm in Essex County, Massachusetts, and the Watson and Casey Farms in southern Rhode Island.

Daily life at the Casey
Farm in Saunders-
town, Rhode Island,
in the late 1870s was
documented by
Harry Weir Casey,
the family's amateur
photographer. He
also took the two
photographs below.

opposite
bottom left

More than ten miles
of dry-laid stone
walls, most built at
least five feet high to
control livestock and
keep out predators,
divide the fields at
the Casey Farm.

opposite
bottom right

The Gould family,
shown relaxing on the
front porch, worked
the Casey Farm as
tenant farmers during
the 1870s. Today
tenant farmers and
student interns help
produce organic fruits,
vegetables, and eggs
for three hundred
families in a Com-
munity Supported
Agriculture Program.

left

Tombstones in the
Casey family ceme-
tery on the farm
record its rich history.
Members of six
generations of the
family rest here,
including Brig. Gen.
Thomas Lincoln
Casey, who helped
build many important
structures in the
nation's capital,
including the original
building for the
Library of Congress.

At the Casey Farm in Saunderstown, Rhode Island, more than three hundred acres stretching from Narragansett Bay to the Pettaquamscutt River were owned by the Casey family from 1702 to 1955. After an initial period of personal prosperity, which ended with the decline of nearby Newport following the Revolutionary War, the Casey family employed tenant farmers who raised cranberries, corn, and potatoes. Family members, who pursued careers in business, the military, engineering, and architecture, retained two rooms in the farmhouse for their own use during the summer. Throughout the nineteenth century the farm remained a firm center and symbol for the Caseys, the unchanging place to which they returned each year to renew their ties to the land and to one another.

Thomas Lincoln Casey, brigadier general and chief of the U.S. Army Corps of Engineers, especially cherished the family homestead and spent his summers researching the farm's history. In his "Historical Sketch of Casey Farm" (1881), he expressed the farm's symbolic value: "[A]s an heir-loom for the preservation of which many sacrifices have been made by my ancestors and as a repository of the ashes of my beloved kindred, the place is beyond price, and I trust will ever be zealously guarded and cherished by me and mine." In 1955 his son Edward Pearce Casey bequeathed the farm to SPNEA, stipulating that it always remain a working farm, as it has.

Most New England farms have not been blessed with the extensive acreage, rich soil, and ocean-tempered climate of SPNEA's large farms. Most were closer to one hundred acres, and New England farmers have always struggled with thin, rocky soil, the challenges of a short growing season, and unpredictable extremes of weather. One of the first organized efforts to improve farm productivity occurred in 1792, when the Massachusetts Society for Promoting Agriculture (MSPA) was formed by some of Boston's leading citizens to disseminate information and encourage experimentation in crop rotation, new fertilizers, selective breeding, and other progressive techniques. In that decade the merchant John Codman, a founding member and trustee of MSPA, acquired a 450-acre country seat in Lincoln, Massachusetts, and planned an ambitious renovation of the house, grounds, and farm operations.

While on business in England in 1800, Codman carefully observed the parklike views, ornamental gardens, and productive farmland of large English estates. From abroad he sent orders that new trees be planted to conceal the barns and the public road in front of his house in Lincoln. On his return he built a new house for the hired farm agent, new barns, wells, and an up-to-date drainage system to support the farm's agricultural activity. Codman was as interested in the property's ornamental landscape as in its improved agricultural practices, planting trees and separating the agricultural landscape from the cultivated area in front of the house with an invisible retaining wall known as a "ha-ha" wall. The response to his efforts delighted him: his wife's sophisticated cousin, Rebecca Gore—the wife of the Massachusetts governor Christopher Gore, who lived in nearby Waltham in another grand house—called the Codman estate "the handsomest place in America."

right

At the Codman House in Lincoln, Massachusetts, the "ha-ha" wall built by John Codman still stands. The "octagon" meadow below it was replaced by a smaller meadow and a pond in the 1860s, when extensive improvements were made to the estate.

The six-hundred-
foot-long peach wall
at the Lyman Estate in
Waltham, Massachu-
setts, is more than an
architectural feature
to screen the farm's
working areas. Eleven
feet high, the brick
partition was built
primarily to shelter
and support the
peach and other fruit
trees espaliered to
grow against it.

left

Alvan Fisher's
1820 watercolor of
Theodore Lyman's
estate, called The
Vale, shows both
the house, designed
by Samuel McIntire
in 1793, and the
picturesque land-
scape beginning
to reach maturity.

opposite bottom

Bountiful spring
daffodils emerge early
in the reflected
warmth of the peach
wall. Riches inside the
Lyman greenhouses
include century-old
camellia trees and
huge grapevines
grown from a scion
brought from Hamp-
ton Court in England.

In 1793, at the same time that John Codman began enhancing his lands in Lincoln, Theodore Lyman, another prosperous merchant and MSPA member, was working with William Bell, a gardener and nurseryman from England, to design the pleasure grounds of his newly constructed house in nearby Waltham, Massachusetts. The Vale, as Lyman named it, was one of the first New England landscapes laid out in the eighteenth-century English picturesque style and is the earliest and most extensive of its type to remain nearly intact today.

Like the setting of an English country house, the Lyman Estate features large pleasure grounds with expanses of grass and unobstructed views, carefully sited specimen trees, wide meandering pathways, a deer park (although the deer are gone), and ponds formed by a dammed brook. Lyman's interest in technological innovation and rare plants was also evident in his greenhouses, among the earliest in the country still in operation today. Here Lyman and his staff raised camellias and other ornamental plants as well as exotic table fruits such as lemons and pineapples.

opposite top left

An 1812 site survey
for James Rundlet's
urban estate in Ports-
mouth, New Hamp-
shire, shows that it
has changed little
since its conception.
The work yard,
enclosed by the
carriage house and
sheds, is separated
from the garden and
orchard, which could
be entered directly
from the house.

Not all newly prosperous New England merchants in the Federal period emulated the picturesque English landscape style. In 1807 thirty-six-year-old James Rundlet, a successful merchant, began constructing an imposing three-story house and laying out its extensive grounds in the heart of Portsmouth, New Hampshire. Carefully planned, Rundlet's garden is one of the oldest in the city to retain its original configuration.

Like many other wealthy New Englanders of the time, Rundlet believed that at least some of his land should be productive. Although his home was located in the center of Portsmouth, a portion of the family's food—vegetables, small fruits, pork and beef, and dairy products—was raised right there. Rundlet also owned a larger working farm on Sagamore Creek, just outside the city, where commercial crops were grown, as well as hay and grain to feed the cows, pigs, and carriage horses kept in town. Rundlet's property was laid out in a grid plan, with straight paths delineating clear distinctions among its various uses: stable yard, cow yard, garden, and orchard. This conservative plan varied greatly from the more picturesque English-inspired estates of Codman and Lyman, showing that changes in landscape taste were slow to affect those not close to Boston.

opposite top right

Spiral rose trellises,
like those first
installed by the
Rundlets, still grace
the flower garden.

Further removed from the influence of agricultural reformers and picturesque gardeners were the many other New Englanders who continued to struggle to provide for their families from the land. Even a minister such as Daniel Marrett of Standish, Maine, spent a part of each day engaged in agricultural activity, growing grain, vegetables, and fruit and keeping livestock for meat and milk for his immediate family. Some people turned to specialty crops, such as sheep or apples, but others continued in the old ways. In appearance, many of these farms reflected their old-fashioned point of view: little attention was given to ornamental planting or landscape design. Barren dooryards, pecked by chickens, were cluttered with the scattered debris that rewards today's historical archaeologist. By the 1830s and 1840s much of the landscape within one hundred miles of Boston had been deforested for firewood, and hundreds of families began to desert their unproductive hill farms for the greener pastures of New York, Ohio, and the other new states carved from the Northwest Territory. Populations had peaked in 1820 in towns such as New Ipswich, New Hampshire, and Standish, Maine. From then on, the upland New England landscape also featured deserted farmhouses and regrowth of forests.

opposite bottom

Adhering to a
straight-lined grid
plan, the Rundlets
planted an orchard
of peach, pear, and
other fruit trees,
as well as grapevines
on trellises. Remnants
of the orchard still
exist beyond the orna-
mental flower beds
close to the house.

Life began to change in the 1830s with a new emphasis on domesticity and rural beautification, the principles of which were codified in Andrew Jackson Downing's *A Treatise on the Theory and Practice of Landscape Gardening Adapted to North America with a View to the Improvement of Country Residences* (1841). This trend-setting book, America's first guide to new styles in landscape design, was quick to have an impact. In it Downing gave a compelling rationale for investing time, money, and labor in the beautification of one's home and garden. "The love of country is inseparably connected with the *love of home*," he wrote, "… and there is no employment or recreation which affords the mind greater or more permanent satisfaction, than that of cultivating the earth and adorning our own property…. In rendering his home more beautiful, [a homeowner] not only contributes to the happiness of his own family, but improves the taste, and adds loveliness to the country at large."

These words struck a chord with Henry Chandler Bowen, an active abolitionist, Congregationalist, and Republican living in Brooklyn, New York, who built a Gothic Revival summer retreat for his family in his hometown of Woodstock, Connecticut, in 1846. Like the Caseys, Bowen believed that his family could absorb the traditional values of New England's earlier, admired agricultural society by returning to his hometown each summer. From the start Bowen placed equal weight on the design of both the new house and the grounds, and he began planting on the property before the house was completed.

Bowen painted his summer home pink and named it Roseland Cottage after his love of roses, some of which still bloom on the property. Family records show that Bowen frequented the Raspberry Hill Nursery in nearby Brooklyn, Connecticut, and relied on its proprietor, Henry A. Dyer, not only to supply plants and trees for Roseland but also to supervise the work being done there. Dyer is known to have worked on the imposing boxwood garden, with its six hundred yards of boxwood edging and twenty small flower beds, thought to be one of the oldest surviving boxwood parterres in New England. The Roseland Cottage grounds in Bowen's day also featured an extensive orchard of apples, peaches, cherries, pears, plums, nectarines, grapes, quinces, and currants.

above

A picturesque garden house adds charm to Roseland Cottage in Woodstock, Connecticut. The parterre garden is edged with its original boxwood, laid out in the 1850s.

left

Henry Chandler Bowen loved roses, planting them lavishly around his aptly named home. To celebrate the American centennial, he donated a public park to Woodstock, filling it too with roses and trees. Close by, it still attracts visitors.

opposite top

Following a ten-
year sojourn in
France, the Codmans
returned to Lincoln,
Massachusetts, to
take up life at The
Grange. The house
and its elegant setting
inspired Sarah Cod-
man's watercolors.

Bowen's descendants enjoyed their summers at Roseland Cottage for many years—until 1970, when the property was purchased by SPNEA. In Lincoln, Massachusetts, John Codman too had hoped that his descendants would share his love for their country home, but soon after his sudden death in 1803 his son divided and sold the property. For sixty years the house and grounds were sorely neglected. Then, in 1862, Codman's grandson, Ogden, purchased the property, which he named The Grange, and devoted himself to remodeling and restoring the stately house and grounds, improving the farm's productivity, and reestablishing the place as a summer retreat for his family.

In 1863 Codman reconstructed the retaining wall in front of the house, built a new barn, converted the "octagon" meadow into a hayfield and pond, planted vegetables, fruit trees, and berry bushes, and purchased hens, pigs, dairy cattle, workhorses, and sporting ponies. Most of his efforts were focused on agricultural improvements rather than ornamental landscaping, but seed orders for some flower gardens give a hint of sweet scents and brilliant color. He also planted a large number of evergreen trees and weeping willows, freely arranging them over the lawns where eighteenth-century specimens of elms and two noble tamaracks remained standing. Codman's improvements at The Grange, however, were halted by the great Boston fire of 1872, which destroyed most of his extensive real estate holdings there and eliminated the related rental income. The family left New England and spent the next decade living in France while leasing The Grange to tenants, who slowly let the property deteriorate again.

After the Codman family returned to live permanently at The Grange, the gardens were designed and cared for by Ogden's wife, Sarah, their son, Ogden Jr., and their daughter Dorothy. In 1899 Sarah began work on an elaborate two-year project to create a walled Italian garden in a hollow on the northwest side of the house. Ogden Jr., who became a noted architect and interior decorator, may have designed his mother's garden, with its fountain, canal, pergolas, and statuary. No detailed plan has been found, but the skillful use of diminishing perspective to increase the apparent length of the garden reflects a talented hand. Its sense of order and classical restraint contrast sharply with John Codman's surviving picturesque landscape outside the garden walls.

Dorothy Codman helped tend the Italian garden and created an outdoor space of her own that reflected the Colonial Revival taste popular at the turn of the century—an informal cottage garden with a profusion of old-fashioned flowers and a carefully planned sequence of bloom. An interpretation of its colonial predecessors, it was not a pure re-creation, for in it she used unusual plant materials that were not available in earlier times.

*opposite
bottom left*

Like her mother,
Dorothy Codman
made gardening an
important part of her
life, not only tending
Sarah's formal garden
but also creating an
informal cottage
garden for herself.

*opposite
bottom right*

The Codmans' formal
garden, although
rather modest in size,
is quite sophisticated
in design. Sarah
Codman never con-
sidered the garden
complete but continu-
ally worked on it,
adding plants and
revising the border.

right

During the 1880s the Hamilton House was home to the Goodwin family, who farmed the land. The large barn on the right occupies the site later chosen by the Tysons for their Colonial Revival garden.

The impact of the Colonial Revival style can be seen even more strongly in South Berwick, Maine, where in 1898 Emily Tyson and her stepdaughter, Elise, bought the Hamilton House and 110 acres overlooking the Salmon Falls River at the urging of the author Sarah Orne Jewett. When Col. Jonathan Hamilton purchased thirty acres here in 1783 and built his handsome Georgian house shortly after, the grounds were soon abuzz with the activity of his international shipping and shipbuilding business. Wharves and warehouses along the shoreline immediately below the house were noisy and often disorderly. There is no evidence of early ornamental pleasure grounds or gardens at the top of the bluff near the house itself, and after Hamilton's death in 1802 the land was used for farming, an apple orchard, and a sheep pasture of declining productivity throughout the nineteenth century.

Inspired by a romantic vision of the colonial past, the later owners Emily and Elise Tyson devoted their considerable resources to restoring and embellishing the house and grounds, working with the Boston architect Herbert Browne and the artist George Porter Fernald. After construction of terraces close to the house, the main perennial garden was begun in 1901 on the site of the old barn, which they had moved out of sight. The Tysons' new "colonial" garden was entered through an arched gateway at the foot of the steps from the house, which led to a path that offered views of the garden, surrounding fields, and adjacent woodland. The garden's dominant feature was a rectangle surrounded by a vine-covered pergola incorporating several seating areas and a small garden room. At the intersection of the main garden paths was a sundial; statues, benches, and other garden features accented the flower beds. Over the years the garden evolved and changed, reflecting the owners' new horticultural interests, their trip to Italy in 1905, suggestions from friends and visitors, and the impact of severe winters and damaging storms.

The care that New Englanders took in placing their houses, designing landscape features, and conserving the natural environment has set a standard. When the Bauhaus architect Walter Gropius accepted a teaching appointment at Harvard University in 1937, he was given a piece of land on which to build a house in Lincoln, Massachusetts, less than two miles from the Codman House. Although Gropius designed a modern house, he took a traditional New England approach to its placement: it faces south, set on top of a small hill where there had once been an apple orchard. Seeking to integrate the house into the landscape, Walter and Ise Gropius planned a "civilized area" with a lawn that would serve as an extension of the living area but extend only twenty feet around the house. Beyond this was a second level with fields, an orchard, a meadow, and, beyond, a wetland left in its natural state. Carefully placed trees were added to the landscape as focal points and to provide shade, and bittersweet and grapevines were added.

Like many homeowners of past centuries, the Gropiuses did their own landscaping, taking great care and time with it. Even before construction began, they planted mature trees in locations that would provide shade in summer and color year-round. Stone walls separated the lawn areas from the more natural landscapes, and the Gropiuses added trellises with climbing roses and hardy perennials around the yard so they could enjoy bloom throughout the warm season. The goal was to integrate the interior and exterior spaces.

Despite the difficulties imposed by soil and climate, the New England landscape has been enhanced by talented people who have practiced agriculture and created gardens that serve as a refuge and source of delight. SPNEA's diverse landscapes and gardens testify to differing levels of skill and interest, varied amounts of resources, and the changing tastes of successive owners. Even today, these landscapes offer the endless challenge of trying to control nature and preserve historic design as well as the satisfaction of creating productive crops and vistas of great beauty.

left

The landscape surrounding the Gropius House in Lincoln, Massachusetts, like the house itself, reflects maximum efficiency and simplicity of design. The four acres include modest lawns near the house, a small Japanese garden, specimen trees, and an apple orchard, all framed by the house's generous windows.

Time-Honored Houses

"Clapboards and brick, wood-frame construction and the demands of the New England climate form a regional tradition which was made a part of the design [of our house]; but it is not a dry imitation of what has been in the past. . . . The Old Colonial tradition of a central hall is pleasant and appropriate today. It eliminates corridors, and from it we can reach every room. The clapboard is a time-honored material, used in the region over a hundred years."

Walter and Ise Gropius, "Time Mellows This Modern House,"
House and Garden, January 1949

The Gropius House in Lincoln, Massachusetts, successfully fuses traditional New England design features—clapboards, a welcoming fireplace, a central hall, and wide, south-facing windows—with such functionalist Bauhaus principles as a flat roof, undecorated surfaces, and the use of industrial components.

I t was important to both Walter and Ise Gropius that their first house in America reflect local traditions of form and function, so they spent a season driving through the Massachusetts countryside, studying its architecture and photographing buildings before beginning construction. The Gropiuses admired traditional New England farmhouses, for both their simple forms and functionality as well as for their integration into the landscape. With these lessons in mind, Walter Gropius began designing their new house, carefully combining the modern Bauhaus design philosophies for which he was already famous with the characteristics of older New England architecture they had observed.

Gropius's respect for the architecture of the past was evident in his use of traditional construction forms and materials: clapboards, a brick chimney, a fieldstone foundation, and a fireplace. Yet, the Gropius House is anything but traditional New England architecture. The clapboards were installed vertically on interior walls, and for every traditional material used, Gropius introduced its mass-produced modern counterpart. His house reflects an innovative point of view in which the old became new. This, in fact, is what has been happening in New England architecture for nearly three hundred years, since the first New England housewrights combined time-honored English building forms with local materials to establish the traditional architectural vocabulary on which Gropius drew so heavily.

right and

far right

The study's double desk, designed by Marcel Breuer to Walter Gropius's specifications, allowed Gropius and his wife, Ise, to work side by side. Their innovative home, a landmark of modern design, incorporates glass block and acoustical plaster, building materials rarely used in domestic settings in the 1930s.

About 1687 in Saugus, Massachusetts, young William Boardman constructed a house that closely resembled the late-medieval architecture of seventeenth-century England. Built of massive timber framing exposed on the interior, it had a steeply pitched roof, small casement windows with diamond-shaped panes fixed by strips of lead, and a large cooking fireplace. Befitting his trade as a joiner, Boardman was skilled in cutting the massive timbers and complex joints of house frames and furniture. To ornament the interior of his own house, he hired skilled craftsmen to add chamfers and stops on the beams and molded vertical sheathing on the fireplace walls.

Boardman's house, although larger than many, had only four main rooms—a first-floor hall and a parlor with two bedchambers above—and a massive central chimney that, once heated, radiated warmth throughout the building. The front door opened into a small entry with an enclosed staircase set in front of the chimney. As was typical in seventeenth-century homes, the four rooms served multiple purposes. The hall was the family's cooking, eating, and gathering area; the parlor housed the best furniture, including two beds and bedsteads; and the upper chambers were used for sleeping and storage. Before long the growing family needed more space, and by 1696 a new kitchen, milk room, and bedroom above the kitchen had been added in a line behind the chimney under a low-pitched lean-to with a sloping saltbox roof.

far right

Early-eighteenth-
century paneling
added to the Gilman
Garrison House (ca.
1690) in Exeter, New
Hampshire, features
bold moldings, a two-
panel door, and no
mantel shelf. Classi-
cism is revealed in the
stop-fluted pilasters.

right

Like the earliest New
England houses, the
Spencer-Peirce-Little
House in Newbury,
Massachusetts, has
gables, a steeply
pitched roof, and a
center chimney.
However, its use of
stone and brick and
its great height, pro-
jecting two-story
entrance porch, and
cruciform plan make
this house unique
in New England. The
wooden extension
on the left was added
about 1800.

About the same time that the Boardmans were enjoying their enlarged house, a building of a very different style was being constructed in Newbury, Massachusetts, for Daniel Peirce Jr., a wealthy and prominent local citizen. Known today as the Spencer-Peirce-Little House, this imposing stone house has always successfully conveyed an impression of wealth and status. In the Newbury area, as in New England generally, wood was the building material of choice because of its abundance; despite the ready availability of fieldstones, masonry was rare because local limestone for mortar was scarce.

As architectural styles evolved in the years before the American Revolution, those who could afford to express their wealth and position through new houses used increasingly formal floor plans, symmetrical arrangements of both rooms and ornament, a rational system of proportion, and carefully articulated classical architectural details. Houses of this type are now referred to as Georgian because of their popularity during the reigns of the English kings George I through George IV (1714–1830).

Such houses typically had four rooms on each floor, often with two separate chimneys and a wide central hall. They were still built with massive timber frames, but now these beams were usually covered by wooden cases, the ceilings were plastered, and carefully fitted wood paneling graced the walls and doors. Larger, double-hung sash windows were used instead of hinged casements with tiny diamond-shaped panes. In addition to being commodious and comfortable homes, these houses were statements about prosperity and taste.

In 1730 in the town that is now Essex, Massachusetts, Jonathan Cogswell, a successful farmer and prominent citizen, married his second wife, Elizabeth Wade, the daughter of a wealthy mercantile family in the nearby village of Ipswich. The house to which Cogswell brought his new bride, later known as Cogswell's Grant, had originally been his grandfather's house. In keeping with their standing in the community, the couple soon decided to expand the house, adding a new kitchen, a broad stair hall, and three stylish rooms. The new rooms reflected the new Georgian architectural ideas, but like other early Georgian houses they still showed traces of their earlier roots in the large kitchen fireplace with the oven at the rear and in the cased beams extending below the plaster ceiling and projecting into the corners of the rooms. The Cogswells' two new front rooms, one on each floor, have paneled chimney walls with bold moldings, molded door frames, and paneled doors. Both these rooms show evidence of eighteenth-century ornamental painting that was replicated when the house was restored; the chamber above has cedar graining and

left

In the hall chamber at Cogswell's Grant, the eighteenth-century taste for strong pattern and color found expression in the painted cedar graining on the fireplace paneling. The original painted surfaces were restored in 1939 by Esther Stevens Brazer.

The ordered appearance of Cogswell's Grant in Essex, Massachusetts, is somewhat deceptive. The oldest portions are the rooms at the left and the broad interior stair hall, built attached to an existing seventeenth-century house that was later torn down and replaced by the rooms on the right. Behind the house are barns dating from the nineteenth century.

green-painted woodwork, while the sitting room below has richly textured green paneling. About 1770 the Cogswells tore down the original structure and replaced it with four more rooms that adjoined those built in 1730.

As the Georgian style grew in popularity throughout New England, homeowners and builders relied heavily on the proportions, designs, plans, structural schemes, and decorative details found in English architectural pattern books, such as Abraham Swan's *British Architect*, first published in 1745, and William Pain's *Builder's Companion*, published in 1758. These books served as direct sources or as inspirations for house plans and architectural ornament inside and outside houses up and down the New England seacoast in the last half of the eighteenth century. Their use reflects a broader understanding of architecture among educated people as well as increasing prosperity, which allowed for the use of expensive materials and nonfunctional details that were time consuming to produce.

Col. Josiah Quincy was clearly influenced by English architectural styles when he constructed his new two-and-one-half-story Georgian home in Quincy, Massachusetts, in 1770. After a faulty oven repair caused his earlier house to burn to the ground, Quincy saw an opportunity to build in the latest taste. Only thirteen days after the fire, Quincy invited the Dorchester housewright Edward Pierce to what would now be called a business dinner. The food must have been good and the conversation productive, for Quincy engaged Pierce to provide a plan for his new house, which when completed handsomely displayed the full range of Georgian details. The window panes, ten by fourteen inches, in particular "excited the admiration and curiosity of the neighborhood." The classical perfection of the Quincy House led to its preservation, almost unchanged, through five generations of a family whose increasing wealth and social prominence could easily have tempted them to make radical changes.

left

A classic example of Georgian architecture, the Quincy House in Quincy, Massachusetts, boasts an innovative monitor roof, one of the earliest surviving examples in New England. Used for conducting household tasks and housing servants or guests, the rooms under the roof were warmed by small fireplaces in winter and cooled by open windows in summer.

Nearly one hundred miles north of Quincy lie the towns of Exeter and Portsmouth, New Hampshire, linked by tidal rivers to towns such as South Berwick, Maine. Throughout this region the ideals of Georgian architecture and design were translated from English pattern books by a skilled group of local joiners, carvers, and cabinetmakers, including Michael Whidden, Ebenezer Dearing, Richard Mills, their sons, and others. They worked in many communities, traveling easily by water from town to town. An exceptional example of their work is the elegant 1774 Georgian house in South Berwick built for John Haggins and later the home of the author Sarah Orne Jewett, who wrote some of her most important works there. In nearby Portsmouth, New Hampshire, in 1784, John Langdon, a wealthy merchant who later became governor, commissioned woodworkers from the same skilled group to build an even larger house in the imposing Georgian style. Behind its well-proportioned facade and prominent portico, the interiors are ornamented with gracefully carved rococo woodwork based on forty-year-old English designs.

After the Revolutionary War, New Englanders broke their formal ties with Great Britain and formed an independent federal government, but they retained their ties to England as a source of architectural design. They soon turned to a new architectural style based on a new vocabulary of more delicate, neoclassical design and ornament that had been popularized in England a few decades earlier by Robert Adam and his followers. Designs in this taste brought a change from the heavy moldings and occasional rococo carving of the Georgian period. In the Federal period a new profession developed—that of the architect.

New England's first professional architect was Charles Bulfinch, best known today as the designer of the Massachusetts State House (1795–97). Bulfinch traveled in England just after the war and familiarized himself with the new Adamesque style, characterized by delicate ornamentation and the use of classical architectural elements modeled on those found in the buried cities of Pompeii and Herculaneum during the excavations begun in 1753. Simplifying this new style, Bulfinch designed several of the new nation's public buildings, later including the rotunda of the U.S. Capitol, and houses for some of Boston's most prominent citizens.

Among them were his friend Harrison Gray Otis, a young lawyer and politician, and Otis's wealthy wife, Sally, who in 1795 commissioned Bulfinch to design an elegant house at the foot of Beacon Hill—a three-story brick town house with seventeen rooms and Federal-style detailing, today the only freestanding late-eighteenth-century house remaining in Boston. Although the house, completed in 1796, was sold by the Otises in 1801 and later used as a boardinghouse, most of the original architectural details, including samples of many of the original wallpapers, have survived. Today the restored Otis House serves as the headquarters of SPNEA.

a b o v e

Federal details of the Otis House in Boston include an elliptical fanlight over the front door, a lunette on the third floor, six-paned double-hung windows, and slender end chimneys delineating a center hall.

l e f t

The wallpaper pattern in the kitchen chamber is a reproduction of one chosen by the Otises when the house was built.

right

The Nickels-Sortwell House in Wiscasset, Maine—with its elegant facade, imposing scale, and elaborate ornamentation—reflects the prosperity and sophistication of the shipbuilding and maritime trade era.

Bulfinch's work was admired by many, including Asher Benjamin, a young architect who published America's first pattern book, *The Country Builder's Assistant*, in 1797, while working in Greenfield, in western Massachusetts. In 1803 Benjamin moved to Boston, where he designed the West Church, which was built next door to the Otis House in 1806. Through his many publications, Benjamin helped spread Bulfinch's interpretation of the Federal style to more rural areas of New England.

The strong influence of such publications is easily seen in the small coastal community of Wiscasset, Maine, where Capt. William Nickels built a handsome three-story house in 1807. The entrance doorway was copied by a local craftsman directly from plate 30 of Benjamin's 1806 book, *The American Builder's Companion*, which incorporated both Benjamin's own design ideas and some of Bulfinch's. The main portion of the house is symmetrical, with a room on either side of the central stair hall on the first two floors and two rooms on either side on the third floor. The impressive cantilevered oval staircase extends from the first to the third floor and is lighted by a conical skylight in the domed ceiling of the hallway. This sophisticated feature was also illustrated in English architectural design books, indicating that Nickels and his builder were influenced not only by American patterns but also perhaps by William Pain's 1796 English pattern book, *The Practical House Carpenter*.

opposite

Light floods through the elaborate fanlight and sidelights into the stair hall of the Nickels-Sortwell House. The gracefully curving stair leads to two large chambers on the second floor and four on the third.

Following President Thomas Jefferson's Embargo Act of 1807, which prohibited foreign trade, and the War of 1812, New England's thriving seaports became less active, and fortunes were lost. Despite the subsequent growth of textile manufacturing in New England, lack of money slowed the pace of architectural development. Simple vernacular buildings continued to be built in the region throughout the nineteenth century, but during the 1830s and 1840s architects and builders began to copy historical forms and ornament in more exact ways, resulting in a picturesque aesthetic influenced by Greek and then Gothic and Italianate styles. These revival styles, which followed in close order and even overlapped in their popularity, can be found in fully developed form in New England, but pure examples are far outnumbered by ver-

left

**The parlor of the
Marrett House boasts
its original 1789
paneling. Interior
redecorating over the
years involved only
the furnishings; the
architectural details
remain intact.**

nacular house forms embellished with ornament in one of the popular revival styles.

For many who were concerned with creating a fashionable architectural statement, building a new house was not essential. One of the most prominent residences in Standish, Maine, has always been the Reverend Daniel Marrett's 1789 house, with its central chimney and tight staircase in the entry. In 1840, however, the minister's son Avery updated the old house by raising the roof to accommodate a stylish new cornice, adding ornamental window caps and handsome pilasters at the corners of the house, and introducing some new interior woodwork in the Greek Revival style. He also added a side porch with classical columns and built an ell, perpendicular to the main house, that connected with a large new barn.

The Bowen House in Woodstock, Connecticut, is one of the finest and most complete examples of Gothic Revival architecture in America. Even its outbuildings, including the barn and icehouse, are all richly ornamented with Gothic detail. Long known as Roseland Cottage, the exterior of the whole complex was painted this shade of pink in the 1880s.

Only a few years after the Marretts updated their Georgian house, Henry Chandler Bowen undertook a much more ambitious project in his hometown of Woodstock, Connecticut. His 1846 Roseland Cottage, built wholly in the newly fashionable Gothic Revival style, has an asymmetrical plan, towering terra-cotta chimney pots, an oriel window, and a full range of outbuildings with Gothic ornament. With its stained glass, steep crocketed gables, and vertical board-and-batten siding pointing heavenward—all features incorporating uplifting moral and religious associations—Bowen's house stands in bold contrast to its Federal-style neighbors surrounding the town common. It is at once an expression of moral virtue and of Bowen's financial success, the fashionable New York world of which he had become a part, and his desire to make a statement in his native community.

In *The Architecture of Country Houses* (1850), Andrew Jackson Downing may well have been describing Bowen when he wrote of "men of imagination—men whose aspirations never leave them at rest—men whose ambition and energy will give them no peace within the mere bounds of rationality."

These are the men for picturesque villas—country houses with high roofs, steep gables, unsymmetrical and capricious forms. It is for such that the architect may safely introduce the tower and the campanile—and any and every feature that indicates originality, boldness, energy, and variety of character. To find a really original man living in an original and characteristic house, is as satisfactory as to find an eagle's nest built on the top of a mountain crag.

right

Joseph Collins Wells, the architect of the Bowen House, may have painted this charming watercolor at the time the house was built. For his design Wells received $500, a commission of five percent of the total construction cost of $10,000.

Although some men like Bowen dared to express themselves in bold new architectural forms, many New Englanders clung to tradition. Whether for the power of familiar association or just lack of money, traditional foursquare house plans with minimal architectural ornament continued to be used for more than a century. Sometimes one room was updated in a new style while others were left unchanged. Sometimes accurately reproduced details from many historical periods were blended together willy-nilly in a completely ahistorical pattern.

At John Langdon's house in Portsmouth, New Hampshire, the Georgian facade and the primary interiors changed little throughout the nineteenth century, but sometime after 1836, following a small fire, the back parlor was remodeled in the Greek Revival style and a bay window added. In 1905–6 the owners—Woodbury Langdon, a descendant and namesake of John Langdon's brother, and his wife, Elizabeth, also a John Langdon descendant—hired the noted architecture firm McKim,

To preserve a link with the past, Elizabeth Langdon wanted her new dining room to be octagonal like the one in Woodbury Langdon's 1785 brick house in Portsmouth. While not strictly an octagon, it recalls the earlier room in both its architecture and its furniture.

Mead, and White to replace the original kitchen and service ell with a new wing containing a dining room, a kitchen, a pantry, and servants' rooms. The massive dining room, the addition's most striking feature, incorporated woodwork made by the Boston firm Irving and Casson and based on Federal-period details in the dining room of the first Woodbury Langdon's Portsmouth house, built about 1785. This house had been nearly destroyed in a disastrous fire in September 1884, but the dining room was saved and installed in the town's Rockingham Hotel, then just being built. For the Langdons, the association of these designs with an ancestor was as important as the opportunity to entertain on a grand scale in this magnificent new room.

This blending of late Georgian building forms and reproduced Federal detail is typical of early-twentieth-century work done in a style intended to be historical and today known as Colonial Revival. Indeed, these basic vernacular forms and details are often adopted and enhanced by builders even today. Both are incorporated in the postmodern style by both skilled designers and ambitious consumers and make traditional New England architecture familiar to everyone.

Regardless of their chosen style or richness of ornament, all these buildings were created to shelter families as well as express the taste and status of their owners. Within their walls, New England families pursued their daily work, prepared and ate their meals, entertained their friends, gave birth, and died. From the local joiner William Boardman to the internationally renowned architect Walter Gropius, the purpose of the house remained the same.

left

The mid-nineteenth-century bay window became an integrated part of the Langdon House, as did the wing designed by McKim, Mead, and White fifty years later to house the dining room, pantry, kitchen, and servants' quarters.

ROOMS OF THEIR OWN

"I like to think of young Tristram [Coffin] as he plied his trade or took up his many civic burdens in this house of his.... There was one room on the ground floor, one room on the second floor, perhaps two, and an attic. Young couples today start housekeeping in a kitchenette apartment, with parlor, bed room, bath and kitchenette. Tristram's parlor and kitchen were one and the same, and the bath was eliminated."

James W. Spring, "The Coffin House in Newbury, Massachusetts
and Those Who Have Made It Their Home," *Old-Time New England*, July 1929

ost early New Englanders like Tristram Coffin Jr. lived in one or two multipurpose rooms, with nothing to separate areas used for different activities. Dirty, smoky, smelly, and wet work was undertaken in the same rooms used for sleeping, eating, and entertaining, sometimes all simultaneously. Windows, if any, were small casements, so interiors were often dark and stuffy. The heat generated by a fire for cooking or heating water could be almost unbearable in the summer, although in wintertime snow might drift in around the windows in the same room and never melt. Several generations—older parents, newlyweds, and young families—often lived together in these crowded quarters. As prosperity increased for some people, standards of living improved and brought more orderly interiors, a distinction between spaces for private and public activities, and more comfortable and stylish furnishings.

Successive generations of the Coffin family lived in the same house in Newbury, Massachusetts, each elderly couple eventually accommodating a younger son and his growing family, sometimes sharing rooms and sometimes adding new ones. The two-story house built by Judith and Tristram Coffin Jr. about 1654, the year after their marriage, had a single room on each floor, each with a fireplace and small casement windows. Here the Coffins lived out their lives with her four children from a previous marriage and their own ten children. Here food was cooked and eaten, soap and candles were made, flax and wool were spun, clothes were sewn and laundered, children were taught and disciplined, ten babies were conceived and born, and two died.

An inventory of the household furnishings taken after Tristram's death makes it clear that the few beds and chests were shared by many family members. People sat on chairs, benches, storage chests, beds, upturned barrels and buckets, and the floor. Family members must have eaten from a common plate or dish with spoons or their fingers; there were no forks and only a few pewter plates. Light from a single candlestick was augmented by firelight, but the rooms were never very bright. Despite the house's apparent confusion and obvious discomfort, the Coffin family was highly regarded in the Newbury community. A tailor and farmer, Tristram served as a selectman, church deacon, and member of the town militia. To his house came town officers, church members, and close neighbors to meet, work, talk, and pray. All lived in similar or even smaller houses.

By the time Tristram and Judith's youngest son, Nathaniel Coffin, was married in 1693, his sisters had married and moved out and his brothers had received some land on which to establish their own households. Nathaniel and his wife moved into the two-room house with his parents, then in their sixties. About this time new rooms were constructed on the back side of the original chimney; a generation later this section, too, was enlarged with additional rooms. By the mid-eighteenth century the house sheltered thirteen people representing three generations. How the space was divided among these three households is unclear, but ownership and control rested with the patriarch.

The growth of the Coffin House was organic, not planned. The extended family added a few rooms at a time, reallocated space in response to the changing number of occupants, and added fireplaces and created larger windows for greater comfort. Not until about 1815, when the Coffins set aside a room as a parlor and decorated it with wallpaper, did they use their house and furnishings as an explicit statement of their comfortable prosperity and long-standing status as church and community leaders.

The parallel evolution of the Coffin family's house and their expanding financial resources was by no means unique among colonial New England families. For nearly thirty years Jonathan Sayward, a successful merchant in York Harbor, Maine, made few changes to the twenty-year-old house he inherited from his father in 1735. In the 1760s Sayward, by then financially comfortable, hired a local craftsman named Samuel Sewall to make a high chest of drawers and add new molded cornices in the sitting room, ordered a set of side chairs in the Chippendale style from a Boston cabinet-maker, commissioned Joseph Blackburn to paint a large portrait of his beautiful daughter, Sally, his only child, and bought wallpaper for the best parlor, where the chairs were placed and the portraits hung.

Before he died in 1797, Sayward prepared a will—drawn up, signed, witnessed, and approved by the probate judge—in which he bequeathed his "homestead, with the buildings of every kind thereon, and appurtenance there unto belonging" to Sally's eldest son, Jonathan Sayward Barrell. (Sally and her husband were already comfortably settled on a nearby farm, so the homestead passed to the next generation.) Sayward also specified that his second wife, Elizabeth, was to continue living in the house and carefully designated the division of living quarters, leaving to her the northwest end of the "dwelling house from the Garret to the Cellar, inclusively and authority to open a passageway from the West Room thro' the bed room to the Kitchen, if she pleases." Elizabeth also had the right to use a cane chair and two leather chairs, reupholster the "Easy Chair," and sit in the "pew where she usually sits on the Sabbath." Barrell was to provide her with "five cords of Hard Wood, and five Cords of hemlock, or Pine, to be delivered annually at the house," and they were to share the kitchen, garden, and family carriage, a horse-drawn chaise.

far left

One of the spaces Jonathan Sayward set aside for the use of his second wife, Elizabeth, during her widowhood was the house's west room. Joseph Blackburn's portrait of Sayward's daughter, Sally, remains where it has been since it was hung in the Sayward family's York Harbor, Maine, home in 1761.

left

In 1770, records show, Jonathan Sayward purchased some blue-checked linen, which may have been made into bed curtains for the first-floor bedroom (left). The parlor chamber is simply furnished with an imported looking glass and a locally made chest of drawers (right).

At the time this water-
color of the Sayward-
Wheeler House was
painted, in the 1880s,
the house was occu-
pied by Jonathan
Sayward's great-
granddaughters, Eliza-
beth and Mary Barrell.

Realizing that sharing living space might be awkward, Sayward offered his widow the opportunity to make a separate entrance from the kitchen into her portion of the house, and she did so. She did not, however, create a doorway between her first-floor chamber and the front parlor, even though she could pass from one to the other only by going through the sitting room of her step-grandson's family, by going out the kitchen door and around the house and then entering the front door, or by going up the back stairs and down the front.

Sayward's provisions regarding the use of rooms are very specific, but whether they were actually followed is not known. Jonathan Sayward Barrell and his step-grandmother may have lived together in harmony, changing their use of the various rooms according to the seasons or some other circumstance. Although the parlor belonged to Elizabeth, the whole family may have assembled there on occasion, as when, for example, the minister came to call. On the other hand, the inconvenience of Elizabeth's access to the parlor may have meant that neither she nor anyone else used it daily. Or perhaps the use of rooms was a source of tension and dispute.

far right

In the tiny entry of
the Sayward-Wheeler
House, the staircase
makes three turns
against the chimney.
Some of Jonathan
Sayward's furniture is
still in place.

Jonathan Sayward was not alone in designating a grandson as his heir. After Josiah Quincy Jr. died at sea in 1775, his father, Col. Josiah Quincy, drew up a will in which he left his new large house and all its furnishings to his grandson, Josiah III. The Quincy House, which twelve-year-old Josiah III inherited in 1784, must have looked like many of the other imposing New England houses built and furnished in the years immediately before the American Revolution: a large building designed with Georgian detail, broad central hallways, and ample rooms with fireplaces occasionally ornamented with imported tiles and decorated with strong colors, bold wallpaper designs, and solid mahogany or walnut Chippendale furniture. In many rooms the color of the curtains, upholstery and wallpaper was the same; primary colors, such as red, were preferred, as at the Sarah Orne Jewett House in South Berwick, Maine.

In sharp contrast to the unpretentious improvements made in the Coffin and Sayward Houses and the bold Georgian interiors of the Quincy and Jewett Houses were the impressive new houses built and furnished after the Revolution by the elite in thriving coastal cities. Acutely aware of architectural styles and fashionable furnishings, men such as John Langdon, Harrison Gray Otis, and James Rundlet demanded large houses that expressed their prosperity and provided an appropriate level of comfort. They ordered fashionable goods from London, patronized local merchants, and commissioned cabinetmakers to provide stylish, specialized pieces including dining tables, sideboards, and washstands. Industrial production of ceramics and textiles in England and their increasing availability made possible whole sets of ceramic dinnerware and a much more liberal use of colorful wallpaper, textiles for window and bed curtains, and upholstered furniture. Families with an improving standard of cleanliness and a high regard for genteel behavior demanded an abundance of bed and table linen, highly specialized furnishings, more secluded privies, and, not least, diligent servants.

above

Eighteenth-century English flocked red-on-pink wallpaper in the parlor chamber at the Sarah Orne Jewett House in South Berwick, Maine, reflects contemporary tastes for strong colors.

left

An innovation in 1760, ceramic tiles with printed scenes were installed by Josiah Quincy in his home in Quincy, Massachusetts, in 1770. His japanned high chest, which he had acquired thirty years earlier, has survived two fires.

When John Langdon engaged local craftsmen to construct his handsome new house in Portsmouth, New Hampshire, in 1784, his intention was to create an impressive space in which to entertain. Only one other house in a forty-mile radius had a double drawing room on this scale, and none had so much exuberant rococo carving. The first guests invited to see this room must have marveled at the furnishings that Langdon had ordered from London: a "Wilton or other Carpet, Newest fashion," four "Window Curtains completely made of purple and white furniture [fabric], or any other color that will be most suitable for the Room which is paper'd with a plain pink paper," four cushions for the window seats, and a "pair of large Handsome Looking Glasses, one for each end of the room." This ensemble was completed with twelve "Large Arm'd Chairs" and a settee, the backs and seats of which were covered in the same purple-and-white fabric as the window curtains and cushions.

For all this lavish display, Langdon's new house was an old-fashioned place. Its most impressive architectural ornament was the rococo carving, based on a forty-year-old design. Neither architecture nor furnishings reflected the neoclassical taste that was already being seen in Philadelphia, New York, and Boston. Langdon was forty-five years old when he began furnishing his new house, and his taste had clearly been formed in his youth. His house was furnished with quality goods intended to last a lifetime and expressed the New Englander's desire for things that were useful but tasteful, rich but not gaudy.

above

A delegate to the Second Continental Congress in 1775–76, John Langdon later served as senator from New Hampshire and then as governor. Edward Savage is believed to have painted this portrait around 1790.

right

In the entry hall of the Governor John Langdon House in Portsmouth, New Hampshire, each staircase step features three turning patterns. The newel post and paneling are probably by Ebenezer Clifford.

The parlor of the
Harrison Gray Otis
House in Boston
features a plain
yellow paper with a
block-printed border
in the "Etruscan"
style, which enjoyed
a brief popularity in
America in the 1790s.

Furnishings in the latest taste filled the first home of the young Boston lawyer Harrison Gray Otis and his wife, the beautiful and accomplished Sally Foster, whom he married in 1790. William Foster had provided his daughter with a generous marriage portion: linen, muslin, and silk; a dining service that included "Table Set China," a "Silver Tea Pott, Cream Pail and Spoon, 8 large Spoons and 12 Tea Spoons," and "2 pair Plated Candlesticks"; beds, tables, chairs, and carpets; and fireplace and cooking equipment.

In 1793 Otis purchased a lot on Cambridge Street and began conversations with a young friend, the architect Charles Bulfinch, about the plan of a new house. The "Large new house" had seventeen rooms and featured both a parlor and a dining room on the first floor and a grand withdrawing room for entertaining on the second floor. The wide front hallway with its formal staircase, much more delicate than those found in earlier Georgian houses, was the space in which the host and hostess and their guests moved between the dining room and the parlor and ascended to the more elegant withdrawing room. The enclosed rear stairway, reflecting new standards of gentility, made it possible for servants to move undetected as their work took them from the kitchen to the public and private spaces on the first and second floors and to the third floor, carrying up food, beverages, water, firewood, new candles, clean clothing, and fresh bed linens and bringing down soiled bed linen and dirty clothing, dirty water, full chamber pots, dirty dishes, brooms, housecleaning materials, and buckets of ashes, food scraps, and candle stubs. Undoubtedly, the children clambered up and down both staircases, blurring the social differentiation intended by the architect and sought by their parents.

below

The Otis House's
entrance hall was a
place of public
parade. New to the
Federal period are the
fanlight and sidelights
around the door and
the display of many
pictures on the walls.

left

On James Rundlet's death in 1852, his obituary described his house in Portsmouth, New Hampshire, as "imposing in appearance and an object of envy to many who predicted with wise nods that so much pride must have a fall and concluded that he had built his house too high—but they happen to have been mistaken."

During the prosperous years immediately preceding Jefferson's embargo of 1807 and the War of 1812, many New England merchants and sea captains in smaller cities outside Boston were able to build large houses in the new Federal style. James Rundlet in Portsmouth, New Hampshire, hired local craftsmen to give his family one of the most grand. Completed in 1808, the house incorporated new cooking and heating technology and was furnished with English wallpaper, glassware, and ceramics as well as the products of Portsmouth's celebrated cabinetmaker Langley Boardman and his contemporaries. Here, too, public and private spaces were sharply differentiated; the enclosed service stairs shielded much of the indoor activity from public view, the privy was indoors (in the attached ell), and the service yard was separate from the garden.

far left

In September 1809 James and Jane Rundlet's new parlor was papered with a "Peach Damask" pattern and a "Paris Flock" border. The original wallpaper remains in place.

The adjoining double parlors at the Bowen House in Woodstock, Connecticut, still contain black walnut chairs from the original Gothic furnishings of 1846 as well as carved rosewood rococo revival-style chairs from the family's winter home in Brooklyn, New York. The stained-glass windows are part of the original decorative scheme, while the Lincrusta-Walton wall covering was installed fifty years later.

Unlike Langdon, Otis, and Rundlet, Richard Tucker Jr., a Wiscasset, Maine, merchant, did not build a new house for his young bride, Mollie Armstrong, when they married in 1857, nor did her father provide their furnishings. Instead, the next year Tucker purchased a handsome fifty-year-old hilltop house and traveled to Boston to purchase furniture, leaving eighteen-year-old Mollie at home with their infant daughter. She must have had great confidence in her husband's taste and understanding of what would be needed, for she wrote to him, "I don't bother myself at all about the furniture, I know you love pretty things as well as I do and that your taste and judgment are faultless. I know you will do right."

Tucker's purchases were sent by ship from Boston directly to Wiscasset, and he was soon billed for the costs of carting fourteen loads of furniture from the docks on the Sheepscot River up the hill to the newly remodeled house, later known as Castle Tucker. Bills from Boston dealers reveal that the loads included a walnut parlor set, a "fancy grand piano with cover," a marble-top center table, a mirror to be hung over the mantel, a hat tree, four complete bedroom sets, a crib, and six sets of curtains and valances. Tucker owned a copy of the 1856 edition of Downing's *Architecture of Country Houses,* and it seems likely that he took it to Boston with him on his buying trip, for many of the furnishings he purchased are similar to those recommended by Downing.

After the family had lived in the house for several long cold winters, Tucker added a south-facing wing adjacent to the kitchen that included a new dining room in the Elizabethan style advocated by Downing. Sandwiched between the warm kitchen and the sunshine, this low-ceilinged room was much warmer than the old dining room. Tucker's father commented approvingly that Richard's "fixings are made in good taste . . . plain, neat, and by no means gaudy and extravagant."

right

At Castle Tucker in Wiscasset, Maine, the parlor set "in good modern, comfortable style" ordered in Boston by Richard Tucker in 1858 still stands on the carpet he ordered at the same time. New wallpaper and curtains replaced the originals later in the century.

right

Redesigned by John Hubbard Sturgis in 1862, the billiard room of the Codman House in Lincoln, Massachusetts, was apparently seldom used. In a letter home, Ogden Codman Jr. disparaged "that dreadful Billiard table [which] has always been an eyesore and a stumbling block. . . ."

above

In 1897, at Ogden Jr.'s urging, the billiard room—"the nicest room of all"—was refurnished as a library to make it "comfortable and nice," as he wanted.

Just a few years later, in 1862, Ogden Codman and his wife, Sarah Fletcher Bradlee Codman, also purchased an old house after one year of marriage spent living with parents. Their twelve-room, three-story house in Lincoln, Massachusetts, had once belonged to Ogden's grandfather, John Codman. Intending to live there year-round, Ogden engaged his brother-in-law John Hubbard Sturgis to make architectural changes, adding porches and redesigning elements of the entrance hall, billiard room, and dining room. For their furnishings the Codmans sought the advice of the noted decorator Leon Marcotte in New York City, believing that he could provide a more integrated selection of imported articles than Boston offered. On November 21, 1862, they received Marcotte's proposals for furniture, carpeting, wallpaper, curtains, and upholstery fabric; orders were soon sent for these items and additional pieces.

above

The Codman House dining room retains its 1860s dado and Elizabethan ceiling designed by Sturgis. The "Butternut and black dining extension table," swan's-head chairs, and low sideboard were ordered from Leon Marcotte in New York.

Later generations of the Codman family did not fully appreciate the stylish Victorian interiors created in the 1860s. In 1897, after making careful architectural drawings of many details of the house, Ogden Jr., a practicing architect and coauthor with Edith Wharton of *The Decoration of Houses* (1897), restored the eighteenth-century paneling and redecorated several rooms. Thirty years later he complained to his brother Tom:

I wish he [Sturgis] had the sense not to try to bring the house 'up to date' but had been satisfied [with] just leaving the design alone. . . . I am sure the old simple colonial paneling and wainscoting was much nicer really than what he and Marcotte did to the billiard room, and dining room, and those dreadful mantels he designed for the bedrooms. But I suppose that in 1862 no one thought anything old fashioned was nice at all. Perhaps if he had left everything as it was I should never have been inspired with passion for putting things back as they were. But that has been a great pleasure to me.

far left

The paneled room at the Codman House features the original paneling from about 1740, painted white since the house's renovation by Ogden Codman Sr. in the 1860s. The French taste in furnishings and fabrics reflects his son's influence thirty years later.

left

After the Codman family returned from living in France in 1884, the paneled room's window cornices, curtains, carpets, and some of the furniture ordered from Marcotte were still in use. The room stayed this way until Ogden Jr. redecorated it in the 1890s.

far right

**The writer Sarah Orne
Jewett's own bedroom
in the Jewett House
in South Berwick,
Maine, remains as
she left it, "with
the chairs all in their
places." The land-
scape painting is
by a friend, the
Boston artist Sarah
Wyman Whitman.**

Similar pleasure in "putting things back as they were" was enjoyed by Emily Tyson and her stepdaughter, Elise, when they were inspired by Sarah Orne Jewett to purchase the old Hamilton House in South Berwick, Maine, in 1898. Their changes to the house reflected their desire for convenient summer living and their respect for the handsome Georgian design. With the help of the Boston architect Herbert Browne, they added functional spaces—a porch and kitchen wing to the east and a sleeping porch and piazza to the west—while respecting the house's original fabric and limiting structural changes to relocating a back stairway in order to enlarge the dining room.

The role of the house in a family's life evolved as New England grew and changed. In the mid-seventeenth century, when the Coffins built their house, the family's most basic need—shelter—was the primary concern. Later, Jonathan Sayward sought to make his home more comfortable and stylish but remained conservative in his approach. By the time New England prospered, wealthy men like John Langdon, Harry Otis, and James Rundlet were expressing their places in society through grand, new homes. As New Englanders celebrated the country's centennial and looked toward the twentieth century, the Codmans, Tysons, and many others attempted to bring older houses back to a romanticized vision of the past. Despite these changes over time, the home remained central to each family's life and sense of itself.

right

**The ribbon windows
on the second floor
of the Gropius House
in Lincoln, Massachu-
setts, were designed
to carefully frame
the landscape, bring
in abundant natural
light, and afford pri-
vacy for the family.**

TIES THAT BIND

"The nursery costs me more to leave than any other room of the house, for I have the most happy and tender associations with it, and I can never have little children again."

Ella Lowell Lyman, diary, 1886

At the Boston home where they lived for twenty-eight years before moving to The Vale in Waltham, Massachusetts, Arthur and Ella Lyman employed a teacher to instruct their son Ronald (second from right) and three children of friends in the house's third-floor nursery.

right

Toys belonging to the Codman children, still at their home in Lincoln, Massachusetts, include "Winter Amusements," "A Fortress to Build," a theater "for the Use and Entertainment of Children in Their Leisure Hours," and much-loved dolls.

far right

Death was an ever-present fact for New England families. Like others, the Goodwins, the owners of the Hamilton House in South Berwick, Maine, in the late nineteenth century, maintained their own cemetery on their land.

New England households long extended far beyond the nuclear family considered normal today. Those who lived together—parents and children, widows and widowers, maiden aunts and crotchety uncles, orphaned cousins, devoted nursemaids, homesick hired girls, and temperamental cooks—were all considered members of the family, whether they were related to each other or not. Their lives together may have been cut short by tragic accidents or sudden illness, hampered by birth defects, or cruelly altered by chronic disease, alcoholism, mental instability, or the infirmities of old age. Family members were dependent on one another for the necessities and comforts of everyday life, and they were bound by the structures of work and social ritual, the obligation of support, and the bonds of caring.

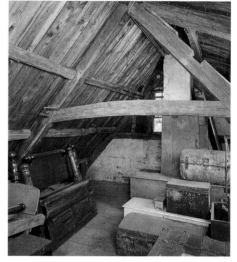

When the widowed Judith Coffin was laid by her husband Tristram's side in the old burying ground in Newbury, Massachusetts, in 1705, her gravestone was inscribed in recognition of her lifelong dedication to her large family: "To the memory of Mrs. Judith, late wife of Deac. Tristram Coffin, Esqr., who having lived to see 177 of her children and children's children to the 3d generation died December 15, 1705, aged 80." In March 1653, when she married twenty-one-year-old Tristram Coffin Jr., Judith was twenty-eight years old and already had four young children from her first marriage. Over the next sixteen years she bore ten more children, their birth intervals ranging from 1.7 to 2.2 years, normal for most New England women until the nineteenth century. Forty-four years old when her last child, Nathaniel, was born in 1669, she was already a grandmother of six.

Regardless of Nathaniel's responsibilities to his own wife and children, Tristram's will charged him to "take speshall care of my wife his mothar to provide for har in all Respectes during her life all things necessary for her comfortabell being both in sicknis and in heleth." With her future assured, Judith Coffin, like so many women of her time, probably spent her days assisting with the care of her grandchildren, helping her neighbors as well as her daughters and daughters-in-law when giving birth, and sitting up all night with people who were ill. During her last illness the roles may have been reversed; her children or grandchildren may have rocked her in a "grandmother's cradle" like the one that still remains at the Coffin House.

Despite the large size of the Coffin family and other families of the time, New England households did not revolve around children. Pride and will were believed to be expressions of inherent sinfulness, so adults sought to control children's playfulness and energy, forcing them to adapt to adult standards of behavior (including not crawling) and to help with the work of the farm and household as soon as possible. The purpose of education was to develop discipline, character, and a sense of religion as much as to impart information and prepare for adult roles in family and community.

above

In the early days some family members may have slept in the attic of the Coffin House in Newbury, Massachusetts, although the temperature may have been well below freezing.

left

An adult cradle and a camp, or folding, bed occupy the chamber in the Coffin House's earliest part. In the seventeenth century this room would have been filled with beds—feather- or husk-filled ticks on the floor—used by both adults and children.

far right

When Jonathan Say-
ward's new desk and
bookcase proved too
high for the sitting
room of his house in
York Harbor, Maine,
he apparently had no
qualms about cutting
off the top of the pedi-
ment. At this desk he
kept his diary, con-
ducted business, and
carried on an exten-
sive correspondence.

In York Harbor, Maine, Jonathan Sayward and his first wife, Sarah, had only one child and enjoyed a happy life together until Sarah's death in 1775 at the age of fifty-seven. Her obituary in the *New Hampshire Gazette* noted the "cheerful sociability, almost peculiar to herself" that had characterized her life and "endeared her to Persons of every Denomination." As the wife of a prosperous merchant who was also a member of the Massachusetts House of Representatives as well as a judge, she had "faithfully and conscientiously discharged the Duties of her Station," serving as a model of religious devotion and charity at home and in town.

For Jonathan Sayward, 1775 was a terrible year. Not only did he lose his beloved wife, but he also suffered serious financial losses. As an outspoken defender of the Crown, he lost his judicial appointments and was ordered to remain in York Harbor. Like many colonial New Englanders whose spouses had died, Sayward was eager to remarry, but the times were so unsettled that, as he noted in his diary, "my mind is so wholly taken up with the distress of my country that [I] have not a thought to spare about matrimony." It was not until October 19, 1779, that he married Elizabeth Plummer of Gloucester, invoking "the Lord [to] make us blessings one and the other." Their carefully worded prenuptial agreement reflects his concern about preserving each person's property for the benefit of his or her descendants. (Such agreements, while unusual for first marriages, were less so for second and subsequent marriages when each partner had property to protect.)

right

Jonathan and Sarah Sayward's large portraits still dominate the low-ceilinged parlor in the Sayward-Wheeler House. Hers was never finished, perhaps because she died before the artist completed his work.

Colonial New England families often relied on some outside help for domestic chores. Many, even those of moderate means, hired girls or women who lived in and assisted with routine chores such as cooking, scrubbing, spinning, and laundry. Wealthy urban families had, in addition, serving men, butlers, and coachmen, some of whom wore livery or uniforms (women servants had no such mark of distinction). A small percentage of the wealthiest New Englanders owned slaves, most of whom worked as indoor servants or coachmen.

Jonathan Sayward owned at least two slaves: Cato, who ran away once in 1769 and was sold in 1781 for $285, and Prince Sayward, who served for forty years before "the new constitution [of 1789] made him free." Perhaps in gratitude for this long service or perhaps because of their close companionship over forty years, Sayward paid the expenses of Prince's last illness and burial a few months later.

In their large household in nearby Portsmouth, New Hampshire, John and Elizabeth Langdon relied for help on a combination of enslaved and free servants, at least some of whom slept in rooms on the third floor on the "good strong cheap Beds, Bedding & Bedsteads without Posts or Curtains for Servant Men & Maids" that Langdon had ordered from London in 1766. Among the twenty contracts between John Langdon and servants, none are with women, suggesting that the employment of women servants was less structured or that before 1787 they were slaves. In a 1789 contract with Charles Herenton, typical of the day, he agreed "with John Langdon, Esq. To live with him for 12 months in the Capacity of a Servant, to drive the Carriage as Coachman, take care of horses, Tend at Table, or any Business about the house whatever." These servants were paid $4 to $12 per month, about half the rate of pay of unskilled day labor in the town.

At least one of Langdon's menservants, Siras (or Cyrus) Bruce, appears to have been an illiterate slave who was freed sometime before 1783, when he signed with his mark a contract to work "as a domestic servant in any sort of business the said Langdon may require for a term of twelve months." Outfitted with a handsome livery with metal buttons and white breeches, he continued to work for Langdon in his grand new house as late as 1797, living rent free nearby in a small house owned by Langdon. It may have been Siras who opened the door when Gen. George Washington arrived to dine and take "tea with a large circle of ladies" at Langdon's house on Monday November 2, 1789.

left

The elaborately carved parlor of the Governor John Langdon House in Portsmouth, New Hampshire, may have inspired George Washington's observation in his diary that "[t]here are some good houses [here] (among which Col. Langdon's may be esteemed the first)."

In Boston, Sally and Harrison Gray Otis, who had begun his career as a lawyer involved in real estate development and eventually became one of the wealthiest men in the city, required much help with their large family. They employed a manservant to drive carriages, care for horses, and wait on table and also hired women as nursemaids, housemaids, cooks, and laundresses, many of whom lived in. Otis also served as a delegate to Congress, attending annual sessions in Philadelphia until 1800 and one in Washington the following year. He was a devoted husband, often writing several times a week and frequently expressing his wish that they could share a pillow. In November 1797, during her seventh pregnancy, he urged her to move into the warmer withdrawing room if the bedchamber chimney could not be fixed. Subsequent letters reveal that Sally was despondent and fearful about the baby's delivery, perhaps because her son George, born early in 1797, had died soon after birth. Otis insisted that his wife not nurse the new baby; anticipating the "little stranger crying by your side on the Pallett," he wrote, "You will not however allow yourself to be troubled by it, but keep yourself calm and quiet and give it to its nurse." Sally gave birth to Sophia Harrison Otis on March 29, 1798. The news of her being "safe abed" after being "ill only for three hours" reached Harry in Philadelphia on April 3.

Whether from illness, accident, premature birth, choking, burns, or unknown causes, many families faced the death of at least one young child. The Otises lost both George and Mary in infancy, and in July 1806 their son Allyne, then ten years old, drowned while swimming in the Charles River. Like many of their contemporaries, the Otises named their next son, born thirteen months later, for the deceased one, and in 1810 they named their last son George, thus perpetuating the memory of the infant they had lost thirteen years earlier.

The elegant second-floor withdrawing room of the Harrison Gray Otis House in Boston would have looked quite different if Sally Otis had actually followed her husband's advice and had her bed moved there during her seventh pregnancy. Although concerned about her comfort, Otis was also aware that this would be an impressive setting for receiving friends after the baby was born.

Harry and Sally Otis shared a loving marriage of forty-six years that endured through the births of eleven children and the deaths of three. "I always knew that my habits were naturally domestic and that my happiness was to be formed only in the bosom of my family," he wrote her on December 3, 1797.

Other families coped with death in their own ways. The late-eighteenth-century fascination with science and the New Englander's devotion to religion coincided at the Spencer-Peirce-Little Farm in Newbury, Massachusetts, in March 1808, when Offin Boardman chronicled the illness and death of his young grandson. On Tuesday March 22 the child, who was visiting Boardman, suddenly became ill, and by four o'clock "Lettel Dear Offin" was in the "Aganeys of Death." While the boy struggled to breathe, five doctors were called in, trying to determine whether the problem was "a sead Swolard [seed swallowed] in the wind pipe" or an infection, "the Quinsey." The child continued in "a Distressin Sitwashon" and great pain for five days, gradually weakening while his anguished family prayed that he be either "raised to health for A Comfort to his parents" or "Releved from pain & have an Essey Death & Rest in the Arms of his Blessed Jesus Christ." On Monday March 28 "at 9 Am the Dear Littel Offin Departed this Life." Three hours later the child "was Opend & [they] fownd the oring [orange] Seed in the bottom of the Wind pipe which was the Cause of Death." Neither sentimentality nor religious scruple interfered with the autopsy, an uncommon procedure at the time.

The family of James and Jane Hill Rundlet in Portsmouth, New Hampshire, grew in the usual pattern, with thirteen children born in the first twenty-six years of their marriage, the last when Jane Rundlet was forty-eight years old. When construction began on their fine new house in 1807, they had five children but were mourning their second son, Edward, who had died the previous January of "Quincey" at the age of eleven months. By the time their house was finished, two more sons had been born, but in 1810 eight-year-old Eliza died of spotted fever. Even within these large families each child was special, and the emotions surrounding death were powerful.

above

The mahogany stair rail at the Rundlet-May House in Portsmouth, New Hampshire, was no doubt an irresistible temptation for the Rundlets' twelve children.

left

The high post bed, matching crib, and cradle in the Rundlet-May House date from when babies were arriving every two years. The crib, moved to Jane Rundlet's side of the bed at night, allowed her to draw the baby into the warm bed for nursing.

In 1894 at Castle
Tucker in Wiscasset,
Maine, an aged
Richard Tucker
enjoyed his rocking
chair in the parlor,
at that time still
containing some of
the original furnish-
ings from 1858. The
portrait over the
fireplace is of Tucker's
father, who like his
son was a sea captain.

When Richard and Mollie Tucker of Wiscasset, Maine, lost their fourth child, Matilda Wood, the grieving mother wrote that she was "the very loveliest of all, so sweet and bright, I never loved a child as well before. . . ." Matilda was buried in the Evergreen Cemetery; her tombstone has an image of a lamb and reads: "Another lamb now safely housed from life's tempestuous weather / Another angel joined the choir to sing God's praises forever."

Mollie, who had borne three children by the age of twenty, was badly affected by the stress of having many children plus an older husband whose "whole aim is to keep the wolf from the door and make my home happy" but who continually remodeled the house, tinkered with new inventions, and drank excessively. Apparently it was all more than Mollie could stand, for in 1879 she voluntarily entered a mental hospital and stayed there for a year, leaving her husband and five children, the youngest thirteen and the eldest twenty. The younger children were away attending school in the winter, but they returned to Wiscasset for active summers of swimming and sailing, theatricals, and parties.

When she came home, Mollie supplemented the family income by translating French books, writing plays from novels, and eventually taking in boarders, but she continued to express her discontent with her lot in life. "When I look about me at the girls of this town and think of mine, I feel that we belong to a different atmosphere—the restless wretched life I have led here from not being contented to adapt myself to these people bears its fruit for comfort in the forcing forth of my young family into a world which speedily formed them for better things than they could have found here. . . . It is far better to be ambitious and unhappy than to be commonplace and contented," she wrote in 1889 to her daughter Mame, an actress.

In 1883, when the
Tucker children were
teenagers, the family
purchased a twenty-
five-year-old pool
table for $115. The
snowy owl was caught
in Castle Tucker's
front yard in the 1870s
by Richard Tucker III,
whose collection
of birds' eggs and
other taxidermy
is displayed in the
billiard room.

The ten-pin alley in the barn at the Bowen House in Woodstock, Connecticut, was part of the original design, reflecting Henry Bowen's goal of creating a summer retreat with healthful activities to engage his children and family friends. At the Bowens' first Fourth of July celebration, in 1870, a delighted President Ulysses S. Grant threw a strike.

The ideal of family life in the mid-nineteenth century became more and more isolated from the world of industry and commerce, and rural retreats for summer living were highly prized by families who could afford them. At Roseland Cottage in Woodstock, Connecticut, far from the pressure of his trade as a dry goods merchant and journalist in Brooklyn, New York, Henry Bowen could participate in family activities, playing games with his eleven children and sixteen grandchildren, taking them for rides, and reading them stories. So sentimental was he about his grandchildren that he had their portraits painted as cherubs and mounted in ceiling medallions in his Brooklyn house; after his death family members framed them and brought them to Roseland.

Attitudes toward children had changed considerably by the end of the eighteenth century. Beginning to understand that childhood was a developmental stage rather than an expression of sinfulness, parents and teachers sought to study and guide children's emotional and intellectual growth. James and Jane Rundlet understood that play was children's work, and they provided books, musical instruments, and toys to foster learning and moral development.

A half century later children were perceived as innocent beings wholly dependent on adults for protection as well as nurture. Clothing styles exaggerated the differences between their world and that of adults. There were more toys, many of which reinforced gender-based expectations for adult roles and behavior. In wealthy families, children were often separated in nurseries and spent most of their time with hired nurses or governesses. This was the case with both the Lyman family in Waltham, Massachusetts, and the Codman family in Lincoln, Massachusetts.

right

Like other mothers, Ella Lyman felt the tug of emotions and powerful ties to the rooms of her Boston house, particularly the nursery.

The Codman
children kept all of
their possessions.
The Victrola and
78 rpm classical
records belonging to
Tom, Hugh, and
Dorothy are just one
of many collections
intact at The Grange.

When Ogden Codman fulfilled his dream of buying back his grandfather John Codman's house and land in Lincoln in 1862, he began at once to create an ideal rural retreat for his young family. Here the children—eventually five in all—had ponies and horses, played croquet, and enjoyed picnics, music, reading, and gardening. A beloved nurse, Reine, who joined the family during their sojourn in France, remained with them for forty years.

With the exception of Reine, turnover among Codman family servants was high. By the end of the nineteenth century, the role of servants had become much more formal. Increasingly drawn from the ranks of new immigrants, especially the Irish, live-in servants were no longer regarded as family members. The Codmans usually employed six servants at any one time: a cook, a chambermaid, a parlor maid, a nurse, and a kitchen maid who lived in and a manservant who came each day. But in 1872 alone they employed a total of four cooks, two parlor maids, and three chambermaids; sometimes servants walked out after only a few days. With a large house, large family, and regimented daily routine dependent on servants, the Codmans employed more than one hundred people as servants during the thirty-three years they lived at The Grange. Recruitment, training, and discipline of these people was a constant responsibility and, apparently, a constant source of disappointment for Sarah Codman.

Of the five Codman children, only Ogden Jr., the oldest, left The Grange to pursue a career and, eventually, to marry. After their mother died, the other four—Alice, Tom, Hugh, and Dorothy—pursued individual interests in music, photography, gardening, and filiopietism, never actively engaging with the world and apparently never throwing anything away.

Above the kitchen
sink, an intercom
phone and enunciator
let servants know the
location of people
calling—for food,
beverages, clean
towels, or other assis-
tance. A button could
be pushed in any of
twelve family rooms.

Fourteen years old
when he began taking
photographs, Tom
Codman became
the family recorder.
Some of his equip-
ment still remains at
the Codman House.

Outside the Codman
House in Lincoln,
Massachusetts, in
1872, Ogden Codman
Jr. and his sister Alice,
ages nine and six,
posed with their
ponies in the drive,
near four-year-old Tom
seated on the lawn.
Beneath eighteenth-
century elms rise
rhododendrons and
young trees planted
by their father.

Like Dorothy Codman, who resided at The Grange until 1968, other unmarried New Englanders continued to live in the homes of their youth. Sarah Orne Jewett and her sister Mary moved into their grandfather's house in South Berwick, Maine, in 1888; Lucy Coffin lived alone at the Coffin House until 1893; and Mollie and Richard Tucker's daughter Jane lived on at Castle Tucker until 1964. Other families—the Bowens; the Mays, who inherited the Rundlet House in Portsmouth, New Hampshire; the Caseys, owners of the Casey Farm in Saunderstown, Rhode Island; and the Barretts, owners of Forest Hall in New Ipswich, New Hampshire—maintained the old homesteads as summer retreats and places for family reunions. In 1889 the Marrett family gathered in Standish, Maine, to commemorate the centennial of the construction of their family home, and Frances Marrett returned to live there after she retired in the 1920s. In 1907 the Langdons reunited at the recently enlarged Governor John Langdon House in Portsmouth, New Hampshire, to celebrate the wedding of John Langdon's great-great-granddaughter Helen.

As family members dispersed in the nineteenth century, many kept in touch with the unmarried elderly cousins who lived on in the old family homesteads. Such was the case with Elizabeth Cheever Wheeler, who frequently returned to her great-great-grandfather Jonathan Sayward's house in York Harbor, Maine, to visit her cousins Elizabeth and Mary Barrell. When Mary Barrell died in 1889, she left the house to a nephew, but after his death in 1901 the future of the family homestead was uncertain. After considerable negotiation, Elizabeth Wheeler and her husband bought the old house and all its contents in 1900 to preserve it as "an ancestral place." The Wheelers worked closely with their architect to provide useful, comfortable spaces for their family, adding bathrooms, a large piazza, and new bedrooms with dormer windows in the attic. They installed new wallpaper and painted the woodwork a "colonial" white but left in place the furniture and historic relics that had been so treasured by their elderly cousins. With minimal change the house became the setting of summertime activity for the Wheelers and their four children for more than seventy years.

New Englanders' ideal of the extended family has remained inviolate since the colonial settlement of the region, when many generations lived together and raised children together. As prosperity allowed, families relied more on those outside the family to help with daily chores and child rearing, but family bonds remained strong. In the twentieth century, even as many family members moved farther away from the homestead, some returned to the family home, pulled to it by its history and the ties of a lifetime.

right

The Sayward-Wheeler House's riverside location in York Harbor, Maine, gave the Wheeler family ample opportunities for rowing, sailing, and fishing. The large piazza they added outside the parlor was the setting for many pleasant summer entertainments.

COMFORT AND CONVENIENCE

"Every time I come back to Berwick I am so eager to know what I can do for it—but the little town is so unconscious of possible betterments, and goes on . . . so comfortably, . . . that it is like a sleeping beauty in its wood."

Sarah Orne Jewett, undated letter to Annie Fields

Residents of Sarah Orne Jewett's hometown of South Berwick, Maine, reflected the conservatism and frugality of many nineteenth-century New Englanders. Although some families accepted new household technologies as soon as they could afford them, others doggedly kept to their old ways despite the potential for increased comfort and convenience. By the end of the century, rustic life was eagerly adopted by some city dwellers during their summers in the country, but as soon as the season turned cold they hurried back to the central heat, running water, bathroom fixtures, and gaslight or electricity of their city homes. At the Hamilton House in South Berwick, Maine, the Marrett House in Standish, Maine, and the Sayward-Wheeler House in York Harbor, Maine, as at many others, old-fashioned technology was preserved for new generations as evidence of family unity, triumph over adversity, and a prudent way of life.

far left

The kitchen sink at Castle Tucker in Wiscasset, Maine, was set in a cabinet built by a local shipbuilder, the water pumped to it from a cellar cistern. The adjacent Hoosier kitchen cabinet, advertised as step-saving, was bought for $25 in 1920.

left

Lamps in attic storage at the Hamilton House in South Berwick, Maine, include kerosene and whale oil lamps, some adapted with electrical fittings for use in this Colonial Revival home. The attic's main lighting is an electric wall sconce with a pull chain from about 1925.

Most families relied on fireplaces well into the early 1800s as a source of heat and a place to cook, even though they allowed large quantities of heat to escape directly up the chimney. Having no alternatives, each year families cut, split, and consumed vast quantities of wood. In July 1790 Jonathan Sayward of York Harbor, Maine, noted that his family had burned forty-four cords of wood during the previous twelve months, a fairly typical amount for cooking and heating in a good-sized house. So grateful was the Reverend Daniel Marrett to receive his winter's wood supply from members of his Standish, Maine, congregation in the 1790s that in return he rewarded them with alcoholic beverages and food: "two pails of grog, a pail of flip, and a supper of baked pudding and boiled victuals."

In all these houses, the large kitchen fireplace with its broad hearth was the center of intense activity. In 1839, when Caleb Huse was eight years old, he had gone to live in the Coffin House in Newbury, Massachusetts, with his father, who had remarried into the Coffin family. Reminiscing about the house sixty-two years later, Huse wrote to his niece Marjorie Huse:

I remember distinctly the great fireplace in the kitchen, which was the room back of the 'sitting room,' and opening into it. On the opposite side was the great fireplace, and at the right as you entered was the Dresser, with its shelves well filled with very bright pewter platters[,] plates and 'porringers'—an article of housekeeping quite gone out, I believe, with the skillet and the crane from which big 'pot hooks' and 'Trammels' hung the 'pots' and kettles—which differed from each other.

The kitchen that Huse so fondly recalled, already more than a century and a half old when he first saw it, was dominated by the cavernous fireplace filled with heavy black iron pots. A large, domed "beehive" oven at the side of the fireplace opening was used for weekly baking; occasionally quick breads and single pies might be baked in a covered iron kettle buried in coals on the hearth. Here in the kitchen food was cooked or processed to be preserved through the winter; water was heated for making tea, laundering, dishwashing, and bathing; tallow was melted for candle dipping; and family members, hired help, traveling strangers, and friendly neighbors gathered to enjoy the warmth of the fire and one another's company. So compelling are the images of the kitchen fireplace in defining the New England domestic experience that enlarged and overfurnished kitchen fireplaces—sometimes nonfunctional—are still being constructed in houses across America.

right

Built shortly after 1700, the "new" kitchen at the Coffin House in Newbury, Massachusetts, features a large cooking fireplace. Opposite is a built-in dresser, or cupboard, used to store and display the family's pewter dinnerware, which through reflection increased the amount of light in the room.

In the huge fireplace of Beauport's Pine Kitchen in Gloucester, Massachusetts, Henry Sleeper installed a superfluity of cooking equipment. This look helped set the style for thousands of museum exhibitions—referred to by Abbott Lowell Cummings as "culinary obstacle courses"—many so cluttered that no meal could be successfully prepared there.

The New England kitchen's productivity and functionality appealed to early-twentieth-century proponents of the Colonial Revival style such as Henry Davis Sleeper. In 1917 at his summer home, Beauport, in Gloucester, Massachusetts, he designed and had built what is perhaps the most artful and widely imitated early presentation of this ideal—a room known as the Pembroke Room, or the Pine Kitchen. Larger than any eighteenth-century kitchen, this room boasts a central sitting area and several dining spaces, but its focal point is a huge fireplace with an overabundance of attractive cooking equipment. Sleeper's interpretation of the colonial kitchen had much to do with establishing the misleading image of the typical colonial hearth still popular today. The Pine Kitchen was frequently illustrated in home magazines, and Sleeper replicated it for many of his interior design clients, including Henry Francis du Pont, whose own Pine Kitchen at the Winterthur Museum in Delaware remained intact until 1959.

Despite their symbolic value, many colonial hearths were replaced in the nineteenth century by more efficient technologies that did not waste fuel or labor. Improved fireplaces and cooking devices grew out of new scientific understanding of the nature of heat and combustion. The most influential inventor of such equipment was Benjamin Thompson, later Count Rumford, who in the 1790s published a series of illustrated essays on the subject. Rumford promoted the use of both built-in masonry ranges with individual boilers and a sheet-iron roasting device in which temperature and humidity could be controlled and kept constant.

opposite

Among many other items, Henry Sleeper collected New England redware pottery. The color harmonies of the redware, pewter, and green-handled cutlery are typical of Sleeper's arrangements at Beauport.

At Castle Tucker in Wiscasset, Maine, an Empire Crawford woodstove was installed in 1905 in the spot where cooking had always been done—directly in front of the kitchen fireplace. The iron door at the right gave access to the brick oven, which could still be used.

right

The Rumford cooking apparatus at the Rundlet-May House in Portsmouth, New Hampshire, is one of the most complete in existence. The round iron door opens into the roaster, in which steam and heat could be regulated by means of knobs and handles; steam escaped into the vent above. The original fire pits and ash pits are behind the iron doors under the adjacent modern counter.

One of the most complete early kitchens in New England incorporating Rumford's ideas is found at the Rundlet-May House in Portsmouth, New Hampshire. The roaster, made by John Badger, and the masonry stove with three boilers, installed by Henry Cates, cost more than $120 in 1808, when a simple iron cookstove might be priced as low as $20. Cooking with such equipment required an entirely different set of skills from working at an open hearth. Apparently Jane Rundlet, her daughters, and her hired help were able to manage this, for bills indicate that repair work was done as late as 1858. By that time much simpler cookstoves were readily available.

Hundreds of patents for cookstoves document minor changes in technology through the 1800s as people sought to improve fuel efficiency, save time and labor, and make stoves ornaments to the kitchen. By the end of the century, the freestanding cast-iron cookstove, designed to use wood or coal, had replaced the open hearth in most New England kitchens. Often the opening of the old cooking fireplace was sealed and the new cookstove positioned directly in front of it on the wide hearth. At Castle Tucker, in Wiscasset, Maine, Mollie Tucker's 1858 Stewart cookstove was superseded in 1905 by the Empire Crawford stove that remains in place today. This stove was promoted by its manufacturer as responding to housekeepers' desires for simpler stoves "at once plain and shapely," with a minimum of nickel-plated trim to polish.

opposite

The buttery at the
Coffin House was
a northern room—
the first floor's cool-
est room—suitable
for dairying in the
spring, summer, and
early fall and for food
storage at any time.

Exclusive Features You Will Not Find in the Most Expensive Ranges—Why Be Satisfied With Anything But the Best When the Cost is So Little Direct From My Factory

As soon as gas and then electricity became available, many families removed their large iron cookstoves and replaced them with stoves using these labor-saving fuels. In contrast, the Tuck-ers kept theirs in place when in 1926 they bought a Campbell automatic rapid electric fireless cooker range, whose manufac-turer claimed that it would save time, money, work, and worry. This small stove has just two full-sized hot plates on the top but features two important innovations: a fireless cooker and an oven in which heat could be automatically controlled by a ther-mostat. Hailed as "the cheapest and most satisfactory method of cooking all foods that can be cooked by boiling, steaming and stewing," the fireless cooker used only "enough electricity to start the food boiling"; it then automatically shut itself off while the food "continued to cook without expense or attention of any kind," retaining heat in the insulated cooking chamber. The Campbell stove plugged into a standard wall outlet and used home lighting circuits.

Without electric refrigeration, people depended on naturally cool cellars, wells, and northern rooms to preserve food and beverages. Butteries, or dairy rooms, were func-tional small rooms, located on the cool northern side of the house and lined with many shelves to hold the broad redware milk pans in which cream would be set to rise. Caleb Huse recalled that the Coffin House buttery was "always as clean and sweet as possi-ble," but in summer, when cheese making was under way, the buttery would be filled with strong odors that attracted insects and rodents. In winter, food and water stored here would freeze solid.

For food preservation, cool summer drinks, and ice cream, ice was required. From about 1860 on, some families, such as the Bowens in Woodstock, Connecti-cut, had icehouses in which to store a supply of natural ice cut from local ponds. Others, among them the Tuckers in Wis-casset, Maine, relied on regular delivery of blocks of ice that had been commer-cially harvested.

below

At Castle Tucker two
ice boxes were kept
against a cold north
wall in an unheated
shed. The taller of
these insulated
chests, a type known
as the Eddy refriger-
ator, was made in
1905 in Boston.

above

The electric Campbell
range purchased for
Castle Tucker in 1926
allowed the family to
cook with carefully
and easily regulated
heat. The drawerlike
lower section, the
"fireless cooker,"
used no electricity
during cooking but
relied on heat stored
in the range's insu-
lated compartment.

Just as technical innovations transformed cooking methods, household heating also changed. Huge central chimneys, like the one at the Coffin House in Newbury, Massachusetts, retained some heat and radiated it throughout the house, but their fireplaces had damperless openings that sent a large proportion of their heat directly outdoors. Rooms were heated unevenly and thus were often uncomfortably warm next to the fire while below freezing against the windows. Doors to hallways, bedchambers, pantries, closets, and attics were kept closed in winter; temperatures in these rooms could remain below freezing for weeks or months at a time. Count Rumford's suggestions for smaller, shallower fireboxes that would radiate more heat into the rooms and for smoke shelves inside the chimney that would prevent downdrafts were soon widely understood by New England masons. Most nineteenth-century chimneys, like those at the Rundlet-May House, reflect an understanding of this advice in one form or another.

In mid-December 1858, shortly after Richard and Mollie Tucker had moved into Castle Tucker, they entertained Richard's father, who wrote about the visit: "[W]e were over there to tea last eve, all pleasant except the cold … need many airtights [stoves]." Three weeks later another family member described the situation: "Richard is very successful in warming his house, has a large coal stove in the hall, one in dining room, and a stove in the north parlor, keeping the air at nearly an even temperature throughout. He has put in double windows all through." Even these stoves and the storm windows were not enough to counteract the cold of a Maine winter, however, and by the end of the month Tucker had designed and installed a furnace in the cellar. It must have helped, for Mollie wrote in March 1859: "I do not think I could live in this house without a fire in that cellar in winter, it is very damp."

The furnaces installed in the Rundlet-May House and Castle Tucker in the mid-nineteenth century conveyed heated air to the first floor only. At the Bowen House in Woodstock, Connecticut, a similar coal-fired "spider" furnace, so called because of its many leglike ducts, was installed in the 1920s, when members of the family first began to live there year-round. In all three of these houses, heat rose to the second floor only by way of the staircases. At Castle Tucker members of each generation expanded and contracted their living space in response to the changing seasons. During the winter months, they closed off the main block of the house and lived in the smaller, more easily heated rooms of the low-ceilinged ell, comprising the dining room, kitchen, and two rooms above, as well as the small first-floor sitting room, using it as a downstairs bedroom.

opposite

In the stair hall at Castle Tucker, the hole made by the installation of a stove pipe in the cold winter of 1858–59, when Richard and Mollie Tucker first lived there, is now closed with a round tin cover.

above

The huge ducts of the 1920s "spider" furnace at the Bowen House in Woodstock, Connecticut, have been severed but once carried hot air to the first-floor rooms.

opposite top

Once the new ell at the Marrett House in Standish, Maine, was constructed in 1840, family members did not have to go outside to use the privy. The multiple seats were convenient— especially the low one for children— but what etiquette or hierarchy governed their use is unknown.

right

The muddy kitchen dooryard at the Casey Farm in Saunderstown, Rhode Island, photographed by Harry Weir Casey around 1880, shows the dangerous proximity of waste disposal, animal excrement, and the fresh water supply. Undoubtedly dishpans, washbasins, and washtubs were emptied close to the well and rain barrel.

Equally as critical to daily life as cooking and heating is the availability of clean water. Most seventeenth- and eighteenth-century New England households relied on dug wells and rain barrels for their water supplies. Wastewater was discarded in the dooryard or simply thrown out the window, and privies were built in convenient albeit sometimes indiscreet locations. At the Spencer-Peirce-Little Farm, archaeologists have excavated a privy located only fifty feet from the front door. At the nearby Coffin House, a freestanding privy was also built close to the main house; apparently the downhill drainage made the site ideal. As the quest for gentility increased, a greater sense of order was imposed, and privies were often built at the end of an attached ell, as at the Rundlet-May and Bowen Houses and the Marrett House when it was renovated in 1840. Like many other families, the Marretts had a three-hole privy with one lower seat to accommodate the children.

opposite bottom

The Coffin House's freestanding privy (left) had good drainage. Still, to get to it, residents had to cross the open dooryard, regardless of the weather. The original single-seat privy at the Rundlet-May House (right), built at the beginning of the nineteenth century, reflects some striving for privacy.

below

J. C. Wells's 1846
architectural plan for
the Bowen House
shows the convenient
arrangement of the
bathing room, wash-
room, kitchen, wood
house, and privies,
reflecting the mid-
nineteenth-century's
attention to the full
complement of dom-
estic service spaces.

The necessity of hand carrying water from a well certainly was one reason for a different standard of personal cleanliness. Until the early 1800s, little attention was paid to bathing the entire body. Most New Englanders used only a small amount of water from a washbasin or kitchen skillet to clean their hands, face, neck, or feet as necessary. At the end of the previous century a new piece of furniture had been designed: the washstand, which held a basin of water and provided a shelf for towels and soap. In the sitting-room chamber (the bedroom above the sitting room) of the Marrett House, the washstand is conveniently placed by the fireplace and is equipped with a covered slop bucket to hold the contents of the chamber pot or the used bathwater until carried downstairs; the pot's contents were poured into the privy, while the bathwater was thrown into the garden.

Bathing had become a more commonly accepted practice by the mid-nineteenth century. Many people used portable tubs in bedchambers, but some houses had small rooms specifically designated as bathing rooms. Remarkably few of these had fireplaces. The Bowen House had such a room, but no pipes led to it. Rainwater was collected in a basement cistern and pumped to another cistern in the attic, from which it flowed by gravity to the kitchen, where it was heated and then carried in basins, buckets, or jugs to the bathing room, much as it was transported to the bedchambers of Castle Tucker, the Marrett House, and many other houses of the period.

left

The washstand and washbasin in the Marrett House's sitting-room chamber were placed in a sunny spot near the fireplace. Family members could be warmed by the fire while taking a sponge bath.

left

Next to cleanliness ranked good grooming. Silver accoutrements line the dresser top in a chamber at the Merwin House in Stockbridge, Massachusetts.

opposite

At the Barrett House in New Ipswich, New Hampshire, a new bathing room was constructed shortly before 1916 to receive this elaborate shower bath with multiple controls that would have sent water all around the bather.

Bathrooms with water closets and running water had been installed in some New England houses, including the Bowen House and the Codman House in Lincoln, Massachusetts, by the end of the nineteenth century. In 1903 Sarah Codman spent more than $3,600 to update a bathroom that had been installed forty years earlier. At about the same time, Elizabeth and George Barrett began renovating their house, Forest Hall, in New Ipswich, New Hampshire, but the elaborate bathroom fixtures they ordered never shed a drop of water. Elizabeth died in 1911 and George in 1916, leaving the work unfinished. The elaborate shower they had ordered was never hooked up to the new plumbing and has never been used.

left

Richard and Mollie Tucker's family apothecary case, or medicine kit, which dates from the 1850s, still holds seventy glass vials with cork lids. It also retains the original paper label listing seventy-six drugs, including five "Diptheria Medicines" and four "Tinctures."

A much larger supply of clean water has always been needed for laundry than for personal hygiene. Until hot and cold running water was available indoors, until electricity could be relied on to agitate and wring out the laundry, and until the used water could be quickly drained away from the work area, the weekly wash day was dreaded, especially in the cold winter months. Laundry was the task most frequently delegated to the help, but it was always closely supervised. Typically done outside in all but the coldest weather, laundry involved heating at least thirty gallons of water; standing in mud while working with lye soaps and bleach; boiling clothes and bedding; rubbing and scrubbing badly soiled work clothes, aprons, diapers, and sickbed linens; paying special attention to small and delicate items such as collars and cuffs; lifting, wringing, and spreading out to dry the heavy wet items; bringing things in before they were soiled by birds or blown away in an unexpected gale; putting away the heavy tubs, wash bench, and scrubbing boards; and being ready to mend and iron the next day. By 1825 some houses had large, built-in kettles that were particularly useful for doing laundry. The rear kitchen of the Rundlet-May House, which is adjacent to the main kitchen and yet located near the well, has such a kettle. With thirteen children born in this family, twelve of them surviving infancy, enormous quantities of laundry must have been done in this room.

At the Codman House a new service ell was added in 1885 containing a kitchen with a built-in range and a separate laundry room with three set tubs (washtubs with fixed bases and legs), a wringer, a washboard, and two pails. Room was also made for two ironing tables with smooth blanket-covered surfaces and a starch kettle. The drying room next door contained two clothes racks, a small coal stove, eight irons, and an iron stand. Radiant heat from the adjacent kitchen chimney was used to speed the drying process, and the stove for cooking starch and heating irons was vented through a pipe inserted into the chimney. At the Bowen House in 1870 a similar laundry room with three set tubs replaced an earlier room in the cellar. Most laundry rooms had windows, and the work was usually done during daylight hours.

For their sources of light throughout the colonial period, New Englanders relied primarily on sunshine, moonlight, firelight, and candles. Because artificial light was considered an indulgence, candles were rarely lighted during daylight hours, and many households relied on only a single candle or firelight alone to extend the day. After the 1789 invention of the Argand burner for whale-oil lamps, the amount of light generated by a single source increased from one to as many as six candlepower, and the use of shades was considered necessary. Argand mantel lamps were usually luxuries, made in fashionable designs of expensive materials. Whether they used oil lamps or candles, few people kept lights burning in hallways or other fixed locations. Lights were usually moved to wherever they would be needed. In the Rundlet-May House and the few others where fixed lighting devices were installed, the flames were carefully protected by glass shades.

For many people the first real improvement in household lighting followed the development of kerosene in the 1850s. Refined from petroleum, kerosene burned more brightly than whale oil and was soon both widely available and inexpensive. Kerosene lamps had to be refilled, their wicks trimmed, and their chimneys washed frequently, but they soon replaced candles as the standard source of light in most households in rural and small-town New England.

Despite the innovations designed to increase comfort, convenience, and cleanliness, few really saved time or reduced labor until supported by reliable plumbing and electrical systems. Electricity was first installed at Castle Tucker in 1915, bringing lights only to a few prime spots: the barn, hall, dining room, kitchen, and front door. The Bowen family relied on kerosene lamps until 1920, when Roseland Cottage was fully electrified. Electric appliances soon followed, with refrigerators, washing machines, stoves, and irons appearing in even the oldest kitchens.

In the early 1940s Ise Gropius found the new technology in her modern home helpful when jobs in war-related industries lured away her household staff. Reflecting on that time, she wrote in her history of the Gropius House (1977):

The standard kitchen and pantry equipment—white glazed metal cabinets, kitchen range and refrigerator, did not ever have to be replaced. In 1938 the General Electric Co. offered us as a present the installation of a dishwasher in the pantry and a garbage disposal in the kitchen because they had difficulty selling these items at that time to the public and expected to get free advertising if they were seen in a house that would attract many visitors. Everyone warned us not have them installed because a maid would always be too fearful to use the machines. They were right in that assumption but when the maids walked into the highly paid munitions factory jobs in 1941, I was one of the few housewives well equipped to cope with the new situation.

Despite New Englanders' nostalgia for the old ways, few relied for long on antiquated technology in the kitchen and the laundry room. Soft candlelight created a colonial ambiance, but bright bedside reading lamps, central heating, and electric stoves, refrigerators, and washing machines followed rural electrification into New England homes as the twentieth century progressed. As a result, houses were brighter and people were cleaner and more comfortable. New Englanders appreciated the clever principles on which the new appliances operated, their energy efficiency, and their thrifty operation. They had been applying such principles to domestic technology for generations—but never with such results.

above

When the Gropius House was completed in 1938, its kitchen—tiny but augmented by an unusually large window—featured many innovative labor-saving devices. The stark white and stainless steel are relieved by colorful pot holders of Marimekko fabric.

AT THE TABLE

"And now they for their morning meal,

Pull out the table, lay the cloth,

And fondly to each other deal,

Some tempting dish, perhaps some broth.

This done they put the things away,

Each in its own accustomed place."

Anonymous Maine poet, early 1880s

left

Jonathan Sayward's valuable and useful silver cann, porringer, and tankard were engraved with his initials so that they could be readily identified if stolen from his home in York Harbor, Maine.

ood was a central part of daily life in New England, a fact captured in the doggerel verse describing Elizabeth and Mary Barrell's breakfast habits in their great-grandfather Jonathan Sayward's house in York Harbor, Maine, in the early 1880s. Even for these impoverished elderly sisters, mealtime was more than an activity to fuel the body; it also perpetuated the lifelong routines of setting up and taking down a table, spreading a clean tablecloth, and finding pleasure in each other's enjoyment of simple foods. Planning, preparing, and serving wholesome and delicious meals have always required much time and energy, but people have invariably found ways to enhance the experience of eating with cherished rituals, ornamental tablewares, and social interaction.

The ways of serving food and the type of utensils used varied with economic and social status. In the seventeenth and eighteenth centuries, rural families expected most meals to be served from a single large pewter platter, similar to those at the Coffin House, and to eat them with spoons, knife blades, or their fingers; forks were a rarity. Dinner was usually the main meal of the day, served sometime in the early afternoon, while a lighter meal, often called tea or supper, was served in the early evening.

As mistress of the old stone house now known as the Spencer-Peirce-Little House in Newbury, Massachusetts, a recently impoverished Mrs. Nathaniel Tracy attempted to keep up appearances. When visited by Alice Tucker "just at dusk" on the evening of October 20, 1789, she was "dress'd genteelly, sitting at her tea table with her children about her." When Miss Tucker visited again a little more than a year later, on December 13, 1790, she noted in her diary:

As soon as we got to their yard a neat looking maid came out to open the gate for us, and conducted us into the house and into the dining chamber, which is spacious and has a genteel and airy appearance considering its antiquity. Mrs. Tracy received us with that politeness which is so natural to a well bred woman. Our repast was slender; two cups of tea and one small piece of biscuit.

opposite

Among the objects in the Sayward-Wheeler House's "beaufat" are six Chinese export porcelain plates in the Imari style. Jonathan Sayward brought them back in 1745 as booty from the American expedition against the French fortress of Louisburg in Canada.

pages 154–55

In 1867 Richard Tucker traveled to Philadelphia and bought a 152-piece gold-banded Haviland dinner set, including a custard stand with twelve matching covered cups. Today Mollie Tucker's prized possession is displayed with other Tucker family glass and china at Castle Tucker, their home in Wiscasset, Maine.

Rarely was a specific room designated as a dining room throughout much of the eighteenth century. It was not uncommon, in fact, for tea to be served or meals to be taken in any of several rooms, even on occasion in bedchambers. Estate inventories, by listing quantities and locations of articles associated with food preparation and service, document some of the ways in which these were used. When Josiah Quincy of Quincy, Massachusetts, died in 1784, his estate inventory revealed that the pewter plates were kept in the kitchen while the more fragile—and valuable—glass and china were kept in the "East Lower Room," apparently where they were used and possibly where they were washed and dried afterward. The tablecloths and napkins were kept in a chest in an unfinished second-floor room. The Quincy family owned silver forks, fruit knives, wine and sweetmeat glasses, soup plates, five teapots, and assorted pieces of the cream-colored tableware called Queensware. The most elaborate item was a glass pyramid, a group of three graduated glass stands designed to be placed on one another; glasses of fruit or wine jellies and sweetmeats were displayed on such stands throughout a meal before being eaten as dessert. The tea table was kept in yet another room, suggesting that the first room was used for dinner and the other for tea. In these arrangements the Quincy family adhered to the cultural norms for people of their wealth and station.

In 1797 Mrs. Tracy sold her old stone house in Newbury to Capt. Offin Boardman and his second wife, Sarah Tappan. Offin's diary describes a variety of entertainments such as one held on the evening of October 22, 1799, when "a company" of thirty people came to finish husking corn and was served roast mutton and puddings before going home at half past one in the morning. The Boardmans sometimes gave dinner parties for fifteen or twenty people on winter afternoons when the sleighing was good. In 1803 they began to hold large tea parties for thirteen to thirty people, and on October 14, 1808, they entertained eighty at supper. Boardman's diary gives no clue about how many servants they employed or whether he and his wife adhered to the custom of separating men and women into different rooms and having their servants pass the teacups and plates of cake around circles of seated guests, but this was a common New England custom at the time.

left

At the Coffin House in Newbury, Massachusetts, as at the homes of many of their contemporaries, the Coffin family did not set aside a room exclusively for dining. The table in the north parlor, probably kept folded against the wall when not in use, could be moved to the center of the room for any meal.

left

Some of the Rundlets' glass is arranged on their sideboard in the "sublime crescents" recommended by Robert Roberts. He advised: "In setting out your sideboard, you must study neatness, convenience, and taste.... I have often seen at parties where I have been attending, side boards and side tables set out in such a manner that they looked quite in a state of confusion; whereas, if they were set out in a proper order, they would make a magnificent appearance."

It became more common in the early 1800s for a specific room to be designated as a dining room and furnished with a sideboard and a large number of chairs. New kinds of dining tables could be adjusted to serve various numbers of diners, and people began to purchase large dinner services in matching patterns. Tea and coffee wares were made of finer and more fragile materials, often porcelain, and tea continued to be served in parlors and bedchambers rather than in dining rooms. At the home of James and Jane Rundlet in Portsmouth, New Hampshire, the "Blue Liverpool" dinner service consisted of dinner, soup, and dessert plates, as well as a soup tureen and ladle and a salad bowl. A porcelain tea and coffee service had teacups, straight-sided coffee cups, and deep saucers that could be used with either type of cup. These ceramic wares were augmented by an extensive assortment of glassware and silverware, including a silver teapot, sugar bowl, and cream pot made in London by Peter and William Bateman.

With the introduction of dining rooms and more specialized forms of furniture and crockery, the rituals of entertaining became more formal. In 1827 Robert Roberts, a black butler who had worked for several prominent Massachusetts families, including Christopher and Rebecca Gore, published *The House Servant's Directory*, a manual of advice for those "entering into gentleman's service." Covering everything from house-cleaning to making lemonade, with special attention given to master-servant relationships and the patterns of service at tea and dinner parties, Roberts's book quickly set standards for cleanliness, food service, and servant behavior. Roberts perfectly understood the importance of predictable service and the prestige derived from a display of expensive tablewares. The principles he articulated seem to have been widely accepted by prosperous New England families such as the Rundlets and were emulated even by people who relied on a small number of servants lacking formal training.

far left

The southwest room of the Rundlet-May House in Portsmouth, New Hampshire, with its original "Green Worm" wallpaper and Rundlet furniture, glass, and dinner-ware, was first used as a dining room. The table is set for the dessert course of a dinner party.

Large, formal dinner parties were common at the Boston home of Congressman Harrison Gray Otis and his wife, Sally, in the late eighteenth century. John Quincy Adams once wrote that in all his experience in America and Europe he had never met a man as skilled in the art of entertaining his friends as Harry Otis. Famous as a connoisseur of fine food and wines, Otis was renowned for his dinner parties. In an 1815 letter to Sally, then in Philadelphia, he described a dinner party he was giving on May 30 for twenty fellow Federalists in honor of Theodore Lyman of Waltham, Massachusetts. Otis himself would sit at the head of the table, and in Sally's absence Lyman, as the guest of honor, would be seated opposite him. The first course—lamb, salmon, pie, ham, soup, and chickens arranged symmetrically around a platter of mutton—would be followed by a course of salads with cheese and bread and butter; wines would be served throughout the meal. After these courses the tablecloth would be removed, dessert and fruit plates set at each place, and the desserts served with additional

The table in the
Harrison Gray Otis
House in Boston
is set according to
Roberts's rules. The
crumb cloth beneath
the table remained in
place throughout
dinner and dessert to
protect the wall-to-
wall carpet from
spilled wine and food.

wines. Tea for the women would be brought to the withdrawing room after they had left the dining room. Such elaborate service implied familiarity with socially correct table manners. At this dinner, Otis invited his fourteen- and fifteen-year-old sons, James and William, to sit nearby on opposite sides of a sideboard, possibly to observe and learn these niceties.

Roberts's guidebook for house servants was only one of a host of cookbooks and instructional volumes that helped Americans become familiar with more sophisticated foods, good manners, and the expectations of polite society. American authors responded quickly to the new demand for advice books. Among the most popular were Lydia Maria Child's *American Frugal Housewife* (1832) and Catherine Beecher's *Treatise on Domestic Economy* (1841), both tailored for middle-class women. Jane Rundlet owned the *Cook's Oracle and Housekeeper Manual: Receipts for Cooking and Directions for Carving,* published in 1830, after she had been married and running a household for thirty-five years; it is unclear whether the book was acquired as a source of new ideas or for the instruction of her four daughters, who were then in their twenties. Sarah Codman cherished her mother's copy of *Domestic Duties or Instructions for Young Married Ladies* (1828), which included guidelines for household management and interior decoration in addition to recipes and remedies. These books and others like them defined for many the nineteenth-century domestic ideal of a home run by a well-organized woman for her husband and children, a home in which most of the heavy work was done by servants.

left

Ladies being enter-
tained by Harry and
Sally Otis would retire
after dinner to the
withdrawing room
on the second floor.
Here they would
enjoy a cup of tea
while the gentlemen
remained in the
dining room below for
brandy and cigars.

Henry Bowen's portrait still presides over Roseland Cottage's dining room in Woodstock, Connecticut. The family's Sèvres dinnerware has been arranged on the traditional pink cloth. The furniture and the Lincrusta-Walton wall covering reflect redecorations of the late nineteenth century.

Dining rooms in such households were furnished with the products of the new industrial economy. At Castle Tucker in Wiscasset, Maine, Mollie Tucker's dining room was well supplied with such articles: Britannia pots for tea and coffee, thin porcelain tea sets with colorful floral decoration, an extensive dinner service with 152 pieces of gold-banded porcelain, another everyday service of green-and-pink-banded Davenport porcelain, a breakfast set, a Minton dessert set, polished steel knives and forks, coin-silver teaspoons, and highly ornamented pressed glass in various colors. Many articles were designed for only a single function. Meat, pickle, and butter dishes, lemonade cups, asparagus tongs, knife rests, celery vases, a mustard tureen, eggcups, and a custard stand with twelve covered cups filled the china closet and kitchen pantries of Castle Tucker.

Knowing what to use and when to use it was a challenge for mistress and servants alike. As testimony that the host and hostess were knowledgeable and could afford an extensive and expensive display of food and tablewares, dinner parties became more and more elaborate as the nineteenth century progressed, with many dishes served at each of a large number of courses. Food and decorations were sometimes organized around holidays or other special themes.

Henry Chandler Bowen, who built the Gothic Revival Roseland Cottage in Woodstock, Connecticut, was an abolitionist and a temperance advocate—the personification of Victorian religious and family values. He and his second wife, Ellen Holt, whom he married in 1865, entertained family members, friends, and dignitaries from across the country at dinner parties, picnics, and, most memorable, their Fourth of July celebrations, held annually for twenty-five years, from 1870 to 1895.

At the Bowens' Fourth of July extravaganzas, guests enjoyed pink lemonade and cake. In the evening Japanese lanterns were lighted, and a barrage of fireworks was detonated. President Benjamin Harrison (center) was the guest of honor at the 1889 celebration.

opposite

Mid-nineteenth-century wallpaper and furnishings set the tone for the dining room of Sarah Orne Jewett's house in South Berwick, Maine. The fireplace opening has been filled with a wallpaper-covered fire board that prevents birds and insects from flying into the room from the chimney in the summer.

left

Marcia Oakes Wood-bury's sepia water-color "The Sunday Dinner" appeared in the 1893 edition of Sarah Orne Jewett's *Deephaven*. It is based on Jewett's own dining room, which has a similar sideboard placed beneath a painting next to the window.

During the latter part of the nineteenth century, family meals also became increasingly elaborate. Table settings were more formal, and starched white tablecloths and napkins were requisite. At their greenhouses at The Vale, in Waltham, Massachusetts, the Lyman family added cuttings from the famous grapevines at Hampton Court in England and carefully nurtured these to provide fruit for their Thanksgiving table.

In reaction to the formal table settings and social rituals of the Boston elite, Sarah Orne Jewett looked back with affection to the simple old-fashioned rural ways. In her 1877 novel *Deephaven*, she describes in detail the daily activities of a New England village. The 1893 edition contains an illustration entitled "The Sunday Dinner," which recalls the Barrell sisters' breakfast with its clean tablecloth and small amount of food. No floral centerpiece or teacups are evident; instead, the traditional dessert of wine and fruit, with perhaps a bit of cake and a tumbler of water, completes the weekly dinner of the minister and his hostess, his sister, Rebecca Lorimer. In real life, Jewett's friends Emily and Elise Tyson made the Hamilton House in South Berwick, Maine,

right

Mary Marrett Dudley (left), a member of the Marrett family of Standish, Maine, takes tea with a friend in the parlor of her Nantucket house in 1914. For nearly 150 years, from the late eighteenth century to the early twentieth century, New England's tea ritual changed little.

a center for summer socializing. Their dinner parties featured wholesome, fresh local foods prepared by hired help and elaborate floral table decorations crafted by the hostesses themselves. Like many Victorian women, they also gave afternoon tea parties for women friends and neighbors.

New England led the way at the end of the nineteenth century in formulating and popularizing a more rigorous approach to domestic economy based on scientific principles. Known as home economics or domestic science, the movement was centered around the Boston Cooking School, founded in 1879 by the Women's Education Association and the cookbook author Maria Parloa. In her many publications, Parloa assured women that their status as household managers would be enhanced if they understood nutrition, digestion, combustion, and the components of a balanced diet. *Miss Parloa's New Cookbook: A Guide to Marketing and Cooking* (1881), a well-worn copy of which is at Castle Tucker, illustrates useful and necessary cooking equipment, much of which was owned and used by Mollie Tucker and her daughter Jane. Another cookbook at Castle Tucker that also derives from the Boston Cooking School is *Mrs. Lincoln's Boston Cookbook: What to Do and What Not to Do* (1892), which contains recipes for quantity cooking and food suitable for invalids and children as well as suggested menus for family dinners for each season of the year.

For some women, education in household science took them out of the home and into the workforce. Such was the case with Amelia Little, one of the last family members to live at the Spencer-Peirce-Little Farm in Newbury, Massachusetts. After studying cookery, marketing, and household management as well as chemistry, biology, and bacteriology at Simmons College in Boston in 1912–13, she served as the dietician at the nearby Groton School until her retirement in the 1950s, returning to the farm each summer. There she and her sisters and cousin took pride in serving homemade bread as well as fresh and preserved products of their farm at parties and meetings of their reading club. At the fortieth anniversary luncheon of their reading club, the members enjoyed "a vast platter laden with slices of cold chicken and ham

and at strategic places along the table were placed dishes of green beans, tossed salad, and blueberry muffins, all up to the usual farm standard.... Dessert was deep red raspberries surrounding a mound of cottage cheese (Amelia's speciality) with cream to add if one wished and—Agnes['s] chef d'oeuvre—a magnificent birthday cake."

For all the new scientific attention to nutrition and the labor-saving convenience of processed foods and new appliances, it was the attractive presentation of delicious food that received the greatest acclaim. Few new homes were built without dining rooms, and at least one had several. At Beauport in Gloucester, Massachusetts, Henry Sleeper designed and had built a central kitchen with service pantries radiating out to five dining rooms, each with its own theme and suited for a specific type of food. Old-fashioned New England fare was served up on thick redware plates in the Pine Kitchen; in other rooms the food and decorations were maritime, medieval, Chinese, or French. Sleeper instructed his cook, Mary Wonson, not to skimp, so meals at Beauport were renowned for their fresh ingredients and lavish use of lobster, wild rice, butter, and cream, as well as for their dramatic settings and efficient service.

At the boldly modern home of the Bauhaus architect Walter Gropius in Lincoln, Massachusetts, the conversation and design of the dining room eclipsed the food itself. The round white table was lighted by a spotlight, originally designed for a theater, that created dramatic shadows, cast a flattering reflected light on the guests' faces, and kept the rest of the room dark. The walls seemed to disappear as the floodlighted landscape filled the floor-to-ceiling windows. Usually only one other couple was invited to dinner, and long before the invention of *nouvelle cuisine* the black dinner plates featured an artful arrangement of perhaps one cherry tomato, a few perfectly positioned green beans, and some elegantly sliced pieces of meat or a bit of fish.

No matter how artfully displayed or how complex and ethnically diverse New England cuisine has become in the last fifty years, long-time traditions and distinctive regional specialties are still celebrated annually on Thanksgiving, as they have been for hundreds of years. In search of the quintessential New England Thanksgiving, *McCall's* magazine sent a writer and photographer to the coastal village of Wiscasset, Maine, to share dinner with four generations of the Sortwell family at the Nickels-Sortwell House. The resulting article, which appeared in the November 1949 issue, included recipes for two menus. One began with oysters on the half shell and the other with creamed lobster in patty shells, but both featured roast turkey with stuffing, gravy, an assortment of vegetables, rolls, pickles, and two desserts. *McCall's* summed up the celebration:

Hardly an American old enough to vote, we'd guess, who doesn't think of Thanksgiving in terms of the old New England Thanksgiving. The bright, shiny November day, the damask covered table heavy with the good fruits of the land, the fine old house rich in tradition and beauty. . . . For nearly 150 years, on each Thanksgiving day this lovely room has been the scene of a great feast. Men, women, and children giving thanks for the blessings of this great land. It is the American tradition at its best, the tradition we should all cherish and remember.

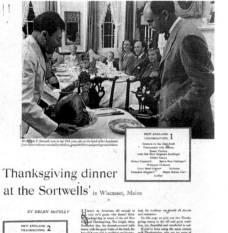

Thanksgiving dinner at the Sortwells' in Wiscasset, Maine

The Gropiuses created a study in black and white in the dining room of their house in Lincoln, Massachusetts. The spotlight on the round white table set with black plates provided a dramatic effect during dinner parties. The Gropiuses brought with them to the new house the table and tubular steel chairs with canvas coverings. Designed by Marcel Breuer, they were made around 1925 in the Bauhaus workshops, where Gropius was director.

left

In 1949 *McCall's* magazine shared with readers the Sortwell family's annual Thanksgiving gathering at the Nickels-Sortwell House in Wiscasset, Maine.

REMEMBERING THE PAST

"How the people of those remote days lived, how they fared, what their mode of life, their methods of household furniture and supplies, are matters of deep interest to us,—if, in nothing else, at least in the contrast of their simplicity and plainness with our artificial methods and manners . . . the day of the shoddy not having dawned either in men or things."

Boston Daily Advertiser, December 16, 1875

Pages 174–75

The writer Sarah Orne
Jewett was photo-
graphed in midcareer
at her desk in her
South Berwick,
Maine, home. Her
novels and short
stories testify to her
reverence for old
New England.

Acknowledging the interest in New England antiquities that had blossomed by 1875, the *Boston Daily Advertiser* described an exhibition of "very interesting old articles" assembled by the Ladies' Centennial Committee and held at the Essex Institute in Salem, Massachusetts. The exhibition's "bewildering superfluity" of authentic articles was intended to evoke admiration and respect for "the era of hard courage and self-sacrifice," those earlier times so different from the modern world. A year later, New England's special place in American history took center stage nationally with the 1876 Centennial Exhibition in Philadelphia. As the several million visitors marveled at the accomplishments of the machine age, they also stepped into the "New England Kitchen" to view antique furnishings and domestic implements associated with prominent families and arranged to reinforce ideas about the virtues and accomplishments of early settlers. In turn, the centennial inspired more local exhibitions, costumed pageants, and Lady Washington tea parties. This memorialization of old New England—objects, places, activities, people, and values, both public and private—continues to this day.

The work of the earliest New England preservationists—the people who kept alive traditions and memories—was selective. A few individuals in each community and in some families remembered the past, identified important places and objects, wrote down details, knew which portrait was of whom, recovered family heirlooms, and told the stories that imbued particular objects and places with historical significance. For memory to live, one generation had to tell the next about the things that mattered.

opposite

Bertram and Nina
Fletcher Little ex-
pressed their under-
standing of early
New England art and
culture in the way
they furnished
Cogswell's Grant,
their summer home in
Essex, Massachusetts.

left

Lucy Coffin lived at the Coffin House in Newbury, Massachusetts throughout her long life, from 1811 until 1893. In 1929 Coffin family descendants donated the house to SPNEA in response to Edmund Coffin Coleman's testamentary request "to memorialize our revered parents in some worthy manner."

The 1735 centennial of Newbury, Massachusetts, was celebrated "in the front yard of the old Coffin House, under the shade of a lofty elm, remarkable for its great size and graceful shape." By this time members of the Coffin family had already lived in their house on High Road for eighty-two years. Theirs was not the oldest house in town, but the current patriarch, Nathaniel Coffin, was a prominent member of the community—like his father, Tristram Jr., he was a selectman and a deacon—and his house's proximity to the meetinghouse made the location convenient and symbolically important. More than a hundred years later, in a small room in the same house, Joshua Coffin wrote the history of the town of Newbury. In 1929 the Coffin House and many of the family furnishings were given to SPNEA.

During its more than three-hundred-year history in Massachusetts, the Coffin family has acted on preservation impulses: the commemoration of people and places, a passion for written narrative and definition of detail, and creation of a shrine to one's family as a focal point. Like many other historic houses in New England, the Coffin House and the family heirlooms so carefully arranged within it are a physical expression of cultural memory, a three-dimensional textbook in which one can read many stories. Not surprisingly, its stories are far more varied than those that were important to the donor, Edmund Coffin Coleman. Each generation brings its own experience to the study of history, deriving different meanings from architectural forms, the selection and arrangement of objects, the written record, and the oral history preserved together in such a place.

far left

At this desk in a tiny room in the family homestead, Joshua Coffin wrote his *Sketch of the History of Newbury, Newburyport, and West Newbury,* covering the years from 1635 to 1845.

Even before the American Revolution, Jonathan Sayward used his home in York Harbor, Maine, and certain possessions to convey to his community and descendants the significance of historical events and the importance of family. In his own large portrait that hangs in the parlor is evidence of his occupation as a coastal and West Indies trader. Next to it hangs a coat of arms painted by John Gore, a New England artist, and intended to convey the family's social status and historical importance. To enhance the family's social position well into the future, Sayward's widow and descendants were governed by a provision in his will specifying that the "clock, a large Map of North America, the Family and other Pictures are to be taken and considered as appurtenant to my Mansion House." As a result, the parlor remains almost unchanged to this day.

As early as 1869 Jonathan Sayward's great-granddaughters Elizabeth and Mary Barrell opened their home to visitors and took pride in showing the "great number of articles worth the attention of those of historical, antiquarian taste." The writer Sarah Orne Jewett knew these two elderly women well, and she likely had them in mind when she wrote of people who embodied "all the individuality and quaint personal characteristics of rural New England." Many of their generation who remained in New England villages were those daughters left behind when brothers and married sisters moved away or those whose sweethearts had fought in the Civil War and never returned. Trapped by poverty and circumstance, these women were often proud and fiercely defensive of the old things and old ways. Using their inherited possessions to define a genteel status for themselves, they resisted selling family heirlooms and even accepted paying guests.

below

Judge Jonathan Sayward, a successful merchant and ship owner, decreed that his portrait remain in his house in York Harbor, Maine. It now reminds visitors of his worldly success and authority.

right

Posing at their home in 1880, Elizabeth and Mary Barrell wore dresses from two decades earlier—a sign of their frugality. Their house was "as fresh as white paint can make it," said a reporter in 1878.

above

In the west parlor of her great-grandfather Josiah Quincy's house in Quincy, Massachusetts, Eliza Susan Quincy left his portrait by John Singleton Copley, his double chairback settee, and his Boston bombe desk and bookcase. For this early 1880s photograph, she added other relics.

All around them, New England was changing. Despite the establishment of water-powered textile and woodworking mills in small towns, the region had lost population since the Erie Canal opened up an easy path to the fertile lands of the old Northwest Territory. In addition, the lure of industrial wages and urban life proved irresistible to many women as well as men. At the end of the century immigrants were arriving from Mediterranean and eastern European countries, and the pace of change was accelerating. The old quiet rural way of life was no longer part of many Americans' experience. Even in South Berwick, Maine, Sarah Orne Jewett's hometown, the shops were stocked with manufactured goods, and the noise of the mill permeated the village. Yet, many people cherished an image of a New England as a timeless place, the birthplace of America and American ideals. Some people began looking at old things in a new way.

In Quincy, Massachusetts, Eliza Susan Quincy began gathering family heirlooms in the 1840s, inventoried the contents of her family home in 1879, and commissioned photographs of the first-floor rooms the following year. When the Lyman family decided to move to The Vale in Waltham, Massachusetts, for year-round living after the death of Arthur Lyman in 1884, they made many changes to the house, but they left the original architectural form and the furnishings of the bow parlor intact; they only changed the wallpaper and added straw matting. Ralph May and his mother were so successful at retrieving family heirlooms in the 1920s that they ultimately combined many of the original furnishings of two early-nineteenth-century Portsmouth, New Hampshire, households at the Rundlet-May House, thus making it appear to have been much more lavishly furnished than it actually was in 1808. In Lincoln, Massachusetts, the siblings Ogden Jr., Tom, and Dorothy Codman pursued the same course, doubling the number of paintings that had belonged to their great-great-uncle Richard Codman and their mother's family, the Bradlees. They hung all these paintings at The Grange in Lincoln, enhancing the interior while making what amounts to an overstatement about their ancestors' taste and prosperity.

above

Ella Lowell Lyman noted in her diary that "we decided against altering the bow parlor" of The Vale in Waltham, Massachusetts, despite making other changes in the 1880s. "We cannot bear to touch it . . . for it is the only room except the library as it was."

left

Emily Tyson and Sarah Orne Jewett stand in the garden pergola of the Hamilton House in 1905. A fellow resident of South Berwick, Maine, Jewett had long kept watch over this historic house.

opposite

The stately elms, the soaring eagle, and the millstone in the garden path at the Hamilton House in the 1920s evoked tradition, patriotism, and hard work— important concepts to proponents of the Colonial Revival style.

When Emily and Elise Tyson purchased the Hamilton House in South Berwick, Maine, in 1898 and set about creating a superior expression of the Colonial Revival style, they relied on the contemporary fondness for the colonial period and on oral tradition rather than documentary research. The Tysons carefully reproduced the original wallpaper in the stair hall but exhibited great creativity in other rooms. For the double drawing room they chose to illustrate in murals the historic buildings of the Piscataqua region of Maine and New Hampshire—a variation of the popular French wallpaper called the "Monuments of Paris," and for the dining room they chose scenes of Italian gardens. They did not use family heirlooms but purchased a variety of antiques dating from the seventeenth to the end of the nineteenth century to convey the house's history. The rigors of New England's climate are depicted in lithographs of winter scenes by Currier and Ives, while Jonathan Hamilton's trade— he was a merchant whose wharves and warehouses once occupied the riverbanks below the house—is reflected in ship models, Chinese objects, maritime prints, and hooked rugs depicting ships. Sequestering the kitchen and bathrooms in newly added wings and moving the barn away from the site of the new garden enhanced the romantic effect by keeping the bustle and smell of everyday activities out of the way.

right top

The garden cottage at the Hamilton House, added in the summer of 1907, provided a romantic retreat at the far side of the garden. Inside, it was paneled with wood salvaged from the Sally Hart House (ca. 1740) in Newington, New Hampshire.

far right

In 1905 George Porter Fernald painted over the recently installed foliage wallpaper in the dining room at the Hamilton House, creating an evocative mural of Italian gardens, villas, grottoes, and hillside villages.

right below

Elise Tyson (center) used the dining room to entertain friends at tea in 1903. The combination of painted "Boston" chairs, an Empire-style table, and shaded Edwardian candlesticks typify Colonial Revival eclecticism.

The dilapidated house of William Cogswell in Essex, Massachusetts, constructed in the early eighteenth century, caught the eye of Henry Sleeper and the great Boston collector Isabella Stewart Gardner as they drove north to visit the Hamilton House in September 1907. They returned another day, thoroughly explored the house, and rescued some architectural elements from it.

Sleeper installed paneling from the Cogswell House in the Green Dining Room at Beauport in Gloucester, Massachusetts. The color was one of the "seven colonial colors" that he promoted.

The Hamilton House's influence on home decoration and garden design was far-reaching. Visitors took away ideas for their own houses, and others drew inspiration from the four illustrated articles about it published in *House Beautiful* in 1929. Some people exactly copied details from the Hamilton House, while others adapted them for their own creations. Such was the case with Henry Davis Sleeper, who visited the Hamilton House in 1907, when he was beginning to develop Beauport, his summer house on Eastern Point in Gloucester, Massachusetts. Inspired by the Tysons' rooms and their installation of early-eighteenth-century paneling in the new garden cottage, Sleeper purchased antique paneling from the Cogswell House (not Cogswell's Grant, but nearby) in Essex, Massachusetts, and began the synchronous arrangements of color and the thematic installations of associative objects that still characterize Beauport. Drawing inspiration also from nearby Indian Hill in West Newbury and historic sites in Virginia, Sleeper enlarged his house over two decades, creating more than forty rooms that were at once expressive of historical and literary themes and suitable for his expansive entertaining style. Beginning in 1916, this house, too, had been featured in *House Beautiful* and other magazines, spreading images of Sleeper's "truly American" taste far and wide.

Henry Sleeper, who posed for an oil portrait by the artist Wallace Bryant in 1906, loved to entertain. His personal charisma and Beauport's fantastic settings ensured his success as a host.

left

The parlor of the Winslow Crocker House in Yarmouth Port, Massachusetts, includes a selection of fine antiques brought by the collector, Mary Thacher, whose portrait hangs over the tambour desk.

The passion for collecting New England antiques reached new heights in the 1920s. Many collectors mixed objects from several historical periods, prizing the oldest most highly. Evidence of handcraftsmanship was especially valued, and collectors often stripped original paint from furniture and historic paneling to emphasize the marks of hand tools. Mary Thacher, an active collector in this tradition, bought and preserved the Winslow Crocker House in Yarmouth Port, Massachusetts, built about 1780, as a suitable setting for her re-creation of an early New England home. To enhance its credibility as a distinguished eighteenth-century house, she brought together a few family furnishings, collected many more of the period, and even moved the house so that it would be in a better part of town.

far left

The warm and homey kitchen arrangement of the Winslow Crocker House owes more to Henry Davis Sleeper than to documentation of eighteenth-century houses. A highlight is a Thacher family heirloom: a paneled cradle that belonged to John Thacher of Yarmouth sometime before 1713.

opposite top

opposite top

The guest room at Cogswell's Grant reflects the Littles' collecting and research interests: New England folk painting, early painted furniture, decoys, maritime objects, lighting devices, rugs, and anything else that was unusual, quirky, or amusing.

A quite different approach to collecting was that pursued by Bertram K. and Nina Fletcher Little, both dedicated students of New England architecture and artifacts. As director of SPNEA from William Sumner Appleton's death in 1947 to his own retirement in 1970, Bert Little was particularly interested in architecture and historic preservation. His wife pursued a variety of research topics and published more than 150 articles and books, particularly in the field of folk art; she was the first to identify the work of many New England portrait painters and other artists. Their summer home, Cogswell's Grant in Essex, Massachusetts, mirrors the course of their research and contains superb examples of the many objects that interested them over the years, almost every one reflecting the Littles' quest for the story of its original maker, ownership, and use. The selection and placement of these objects in the rooms at Cogswell's Grant were never intended to re-create actual eighteenth-century interiors but were governed by sophisticated attention to color and form, the intrinsic relationships of objects to one another, the Littles' definition of what was suitable for an eighteenth-century New England farmhouse, and the needs of comfortable summer living for their family and friends.

right

In Nina Fletcher Little's tiny office at Cogswell's Grant in Essex, Massachusetts, she catalogued her collections, kept farm accounts, and pursued a voluminous correspondence with students, collectors, and antiques dealers. Favorite decoys and research books fill the shelves.

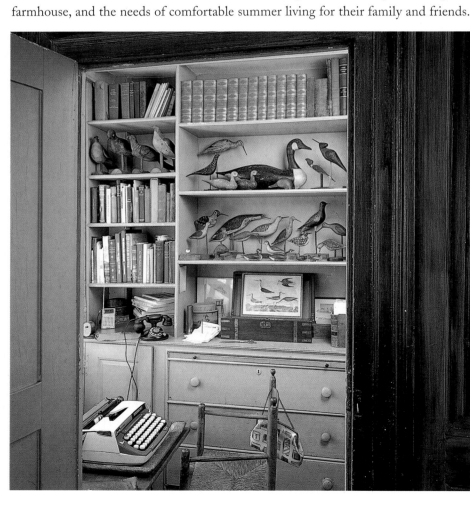

opposite bottom

As Sarah Orne Jewett described a typical New England attic in *Deephaven*, the Littles' attic was a place where "nothing seems to have been thrown away." Treasured boxes range from a rare seventeenth-century blanket chest (left), heavily used but never restored, to an unused coffin (right).

Since these owners began to save their own memories of New England, approaches to preservation and the interpretation of historic places have changed. SPNEA's own goal in the past ninety years, as it continues the work of these earlier preservationists, has always been to preserve its historic properties for research and enjoyment now and in the future. William Sumner Appleton was particularly interested in showing a building's original appearance and saving as much of the original materials as possible, but he was not averse to aggressive restoration—that is, reproducing lost architectural elements, wallpaper, furnishing schemes, and decorative treatments to fill out the picture and achieve the desired effect. His decisions were based on meticulous scholarship and carefully documented with photographs and written notes. SPNEA's most ambitious restoration project during his tenure was the 1698 Browne House in Watertown, Massachusetts.

Although they preserved Beauport intact, Appleton's successors, Bertram Little and Abbott Lowell Cummings, undertook aggressive restoration of earlier houses, carefully documenting their work in removing Victorian porches at the Casey Farm in Saunderstown, Rhode Island; taking down the wings that housed Emily Tyson's kitchen and sleeping porches at the Hamilton House in South Berwick, Maine; exposing the stone end and replacing the casement windows at the Arnold House in Lincoln, Rhode Island, built about 1687; and meticulously re-creating the first wallpapers, original paint colors, and an appropriate furnishing plan for the Harrison Gray Otis House in Boston. The impulse to replicate the original appearance of houses was largely abandoned, however, as SPNEA became the owner of several properties with thousands of family objects assembled over many generations and decorative schemes that illustrated change through the years. Now, consistently using a more comprehensive approach to preservation, the organization's goal is to preserve the appearance and arrangement of a property at the time it is acquired or when last lived in and cared for by its owners, rather than restore it to some earlier moment in the past.

SPNEA's acquisition of its first Victorian building complex, the 1846 Roseland Cottage in Woodstock, Connecticut, together with many of its original family furnishings and a rich accumulation of nineteenth-century material, opened the door for conversations and negotiations with Ise Gropius, the widow of Walter Gropius. Their twentieth-century landmark, completed in 1938, soon came under SPNEA's umbrella, along with all of its furnishings, art, and personal effects. Such properties represent many layers of history and offer multiple interpretations, proving that the pool of things worth saving is much broader than the colonial.

Each generation's perception of the past is filtered through its own experience, its memories, and the preservation activities of those who have come before—by people such as Elizabeth and Mary Barrell in York Harbor, Maine, who kept their great-grandfather's house sacrosanct; Sarah Orne Jewett, who penned an indelible impression of New England; and the many self-appointed family historians and owners who have tried to reflect the past in their homes. Yet evidence of old ways and old values remains reassuring. Those things that served New Englanders well in the face of earlier hardships offer continuing hope for coping with the complexities of contemporary life and the accelerating pace of social change.

Arnold House Ⓢ
ca. 1687
487 Great Road
Lincoln, R.I. 02865
(617) 227-3956

Boardman House Ⓢ
ca. 1687
17 Howard Street
Saugus, Mass. 01906
(617) 227-3956

Barrett House
(Forest Hall)
ca. 1800
Main Street
New Ipswich, N.H.
03071
(603) 878-2517

Bowen House
(Roseland Cottage)
1846
Route 169
Woodstock, Conn.
06281
(860) 928-4074

Beauport (Sleeper-
McCann House)
1907–34
75 Eastern Point
Boulevard
Gloucester, Mass.
01930
(978) 283-0800

Browne House Ⓢ
ca. 1698
562 Main Street
Watertown, Mass.
02172
(617) 227-3956

Casey Farm
ca. 1750
2325 Boston Neck
Road
Saunderstown, R.I.
02874
(401) 295-1030

Codman House
(The Grange)
ca. 1740
Codman Road
Lincoln, Mass. 01773
(781) 259-8843

Castle Tucker
1807
Lee Street at
High Street
Wiscasset, Maine
04578
(603) 436-3205

Coffin House
ca. 1654
14 High Road
(Route 1A)
Newbury, Mass.
01951
(978) 462-2634

Clemence-Irons
House ⑤
ca. 1680
38 George Waterman
Road
Johnston, R.I. 02919
(617) 227-3956

Cogswell's Grant
ca. 1730
Spring Street
Essex, Mass. 01929
(978) 768-3632

Cooper-Frost-Austin
House Ⓢ
ca. 1690
21 Linnaean Street
Cambridge, Mass.
02138
(617) 227-3956

Gedney House Ⓢ
1665
21 High Street
Salem, Mass. 01970
(617) 227-3956

Winslow Crocker
House
ca. 1780
250 Route 6A
(Old King's Highway)
Yarmouth Port, Mass.
02675
(508) 362-4385

Gilman Garrison
House
ca. 1690
12 Water Street
Exeter, N.H. 03833
(603) 436-3205

Dole-Little House Ⓢ
ca. 1715
289 High Road
Newbury, Mass.
01951
(978) 462-2634

Gropius House
1938
68 Baker Bridge Road
Lincoln, Mass. 01773
(781) 259-8098

Hamilton House
ca. 1785
40 Vaughan's Lane
South Berwick, Maine
03908
(207) 384-2454

Governor John
Langdon House
1784
143 Pleasant Street
Portsmouth, N.H.
03801
(603) 436-3205

Jackson House
ca. 1664
76 Northwest Street
Portsmouth, N.H.
03801
(603) 436-3205

Lyman Estate
(The Vale)
1793
185 Lyman Street
Waltham, Mass.
02452
(781) 891-1985

Sarah Orne Jewett
House
1774
5 Portland Street
South Berwick, Maine
03908
(207) 384-2454

Marrett House
1789
Route 25
Standish, Maine
04084
(207) 642-3032

Merwin House
(Tranquility)
ca. 1825
14 Main Street
Stockbridge, Mass.
01262
(413) 298-4703

Pierce House Ⓢ
ca. 1650
24 Oakton Avenue
Dorchester, Mass.
02122
(617) 227-3956

Nickels-Sortwell
House
1807
12 Main Street
(Route 1)
Wiscasset, Maine
04578
(207) 882-6218

Quincy House
1770
20 Muirhead Street
Quincy, Mass. 02170
(617) 471-4508

Harrison Gray Otis
House
1796
141 Cambridge Street
Boston, Mass. 02114
(617) 227-3956

Rocky Hill Meeting
House Ⓢ
1785
4 Portsmouth Road
Amesbury, Mass.
01913
(978) 462-2634

Rundlet-May House
1807
364 Middle Street
Portsmouth, N.H.
03801
(603) 436-3205

Swett-Ilsley House Ⓢ
ca. 1670
4 High Road
Newbury, Mass.
01951
(978) 462-2634

Sayward-Wheeler
House
ca. 1718
79 Barrell Lane
Extension
York Harbor, Maine
03911
(603) 436-3205

Watson Farm
ca. 1796
455 North Road
Jamestown, R.I.
02835
(401) 423-0005

Spencer-Peirce-Little
Farm
ca. 1690
5 Little's Lane
Newbury, Mass.
01951
(978) 462-2634

Ⓢ Properties marked
with this symbol are
study houses and are
open to the public
by appointment only.
House museums are
open June 1–October
15 or year-round. For
more information,
visit SPNEA's web site
at www.spnea.org.

Blanchard, Paula. *Sarah Orne Jewett: Her World and Her Work*. Reading, Mass.: Addison-Wesley, 1994.

"The Codman Estate." Edited by Abbott Lowell Cummings. *Old-Time New England* 71, no. 258 (1981).

Cowan, Ruth Schwartz. *More Work for Mother: The Ironies of Household Technology from the Open Hearth to the Microwave*. New York: Basic Books, 1983.

Cummings, Abbott Lowell. *Architecture in Early New England*. 1958. Rev. ed. Sturbridge, Mass.: Old Sturbridge Village, 1984.

Curtis, Nancy, and Nylander, Richard C. *Beauport*. SPNEA. Boston: David R. Godine, 1990.

Downing, Andrew Jackson. *The Architecture of Country Houses*. 1859. Reprint, New York: Dover Publications, 1969.

Emmet, Alan. *So Fine a Prospect: Historic New England Gardens*. Hanover, N.H.: University Press of New England, 1996.

Giffen, Sarah L., and Murphy, Kevin D., eds. *A Noble and Dignified Stream: The Piscataqua Region in the Colonial Revival*. York, Maine: Old York Historical Society, 1992.

Gropius, Ise. *Gropius House: A History by Ise Gropius*. Boston: SPNEA, 1977.

Handlin, David P. *The American Home: Architecture and Society, 1815–1915*. Boston: Little, Brown, 1979.

Hosmer, Charles. *Presence of the Past: A History of the Preservation Movement in the United States Before Williamsburg*. New York: Putnam, 1965.

Jewett, Sarah Orne. *Deephaven*. 1877. Reprint, Portsmouth, N.H.: Peter E. Randall, Old Berwick Historical Society, 1993.

Little, Nina Fletcher. *Country Arts in Early American Homes*. 1975. Rev. ed. Boston: SPNEA, 1999.
——— . *Little by Little: Six Decades of Collecting American Decorative Arts*. 1984. Rev. ed. Boston: SPNEA, 1998.

Morison, Samuel Eliot. *Harrison Gray Otis, 1765–1848: The Urbane Federalist*. Boston: Houghton Mifflin, 1969.

Nylander, Jane C. *Our Own Snug Fireside: Images of the New England Home, 1760-1860*. New Haven, Conn.: Yale University Press, 1983.

Roberts, Robert. *The House Servant's Directory*. 1827. Reprint, Armonk, N.Y.: M. E. Sharpe, 1998.

Stein, Roger B., and Truettner, William H., eds. *Picturing Old New England: Image and Memory*. National Museum of American Art, Smithsonian Institution. New Haven, Conn.: Yale University Press, 1999.

Williams, Susan. *Savory Suppers and Fashionable Feasts: Dining in Victorian America*. New York: Pantheon Books, 1985.

Like many books, *Windows on the Past* represents the inspiration and collaboration of many people, none more important than those who created and cherished homes in the historic houses now belonging to the Society for the Preservation of New England Antiquities. Through four centuries these New Englanders worked their land, built their houses, redecorated their interiors, rearranged their furniture, displayed their keepsakes, and preserved the things that now make up SPNEA's extraordinarily rich collection. We are indebted to all of them for preserving these treasures and placing them in our hands.

As it illustrates these treasures and earlier lifestyles, the book also reflects the talent and commitment of the SPNEA staff through the years: the discerning collecting and fine scholarship of William Sumner Appleton, Bertram K. Little, and Abbott Lowell Cummings, as well as the responsible stewardship of Nancy Coolidge and all those who have served SPNEA as trustees. We are especially grateful to the current trustees and notably Robert Owens, chair, for their support of this project.

The book's original concept and organizing themes were developed by Kenneth Ames, who unfortunately was unable to complete the project. As coauthors, we have worked closely with a staff publication committee that has suggested themes and illustration topics, provided research information, and reviewed text. We thank each of them: Nancy Carlisle, Peter Gittleman, Anne Grady, and Richard Nylander. Other SPNEA staff members who were especially helpful include Rebecca Aaronson, Kathi Gellar, Betsy Igleheart, Melinda Linderer, Laura Roberts, Jennifer Swope, John Tarvin, and Bill Tramposch. The assistance of Lorna Condon, archivist and publication committee member, was invaluable, and Joan Kertis provided important additional support.

The book owes much to Diane Maddex of Archetype Press, whose idea it was to publish it; to Gretchen Smith Mui, editor; and to Robert L. Wiser, designer. We appreciate the many ways in which they have brought clarity to our work and improved its appearance. Any faults in the text, however, remain entirely our own.

The glory of this book is certainly its photographs, and for those we thank David Bohl, who was SPNEA's photographer for twenty-three years. Drawing on his long experience in observing these properties, he took seriously our charge to show them in ways never seen before. He capitalized on dawn's early light and twilight's last hour, enjoyed glorious summer days, and undertook many hasty drives to catch a view before fresh snow was marred or melted. For his talent and determination to make this a beautiful book, we are indeed grateful. Our contribution pales next to his.

Writing as coauthors is often not an easy task, but we have found harmony in our perceptions of the way to share ideas and images. Further, we have found loving support at home, and for that we wish to thank Tom Giffen, Sarah Rooker, Carl and Gary Viera, and Timothy and Richard Nylander.

Jane C. Nylander and Diane L. Viera

Page numbers in italics indicate illustrations.

Adam, Robert, 71
Adams, John, 9
Adams, John Quincy, 162
The American Builder's Companion (Benjamin), 72
Andrew, A. Piatt, *171*
Appleton, William Sumner, 10, 12, 14, 15, 63, 194, 196, 197
The Architecture of Country Houses (Downing), 76, 96
Arnold House, 197, *198*

Badger, John, 136
Barrell, Elizabeth and Mary, 86, 126, 156, 167, 180, *181*, 197
Barrett, George and Elizabeth, family, 124, 147
Barrett House (Forest Hall), *7, 9, 27, 33,* 124, *146,* 147, *150, 198*
Bateman, Peter and William, 161
Bauhaus, 15, 57, 60, 172, 197
Beauport (Sleeper-McCann House), *16, 134,* 135, *135, 170,* 171, *171, 188,* 189, 190, *191,* 197, *198*
Beecher, Catharine, 163

Bell, William, 47
Benjamin, Asher, 72
Blackburn, Joseph, 85
The Blithedale Romance (Hawthorne), 32
Boardman, Langley, 95
Boardman, Offin, Sr., family, 117, 159
Boardman, William, family, 63, 64, 79
Boardman (William) House, *62,* 63, *63, 198*
Bolton, Charles, 14
Boston Daily Advertiser, 174, 176
Bowen, Henry Chandler and Ellen, family, 15, 51, 52, 76, 120, 124, 138, 152, 164, *165*
Bowen House (Roseland Cottage), 15, *30, 50–51,* 51, 52, 76, *76, 76–77, 96–97,* 120, *120–21,* 141, *141,* 142, 145, *145,* 147, 148, 152, 164, *164, 165,* 197, *198*
Bradlee family, 183
Brazer, Esther Stevens, 66
Breuer, Marcel, 60, 172
The British Architect (Swan), 67, 68
Browne, Herbert, 54, 102
Browne House, 196, *198*

The Builder's Companion (Pain), 67
Bulfinch, Charles, 71, 72, 93
Bulletin of the Society for the Preservation of New England Antiquities, 12, 14
Byron, Lord, 190

Casey, Thomas Lincoln, 43
Casey family, 43, 51, 124, 142
Casey Farm, 26, 40, 42, 43, *43,* 124, 142, 197, *199*
Castle Tucker, *28, 34,* 40, 96, *96,* 118, *118–19, 130–31,* 136, *136–37,* 138, *138, 140,* 141, 145, 151, 152, *154–55,* 164, 168, *199*
Cates, Henry, 136
Centennial Exhibition (1876), 176
Child, Lydia Maria, 163
Clemence-Irons House, *199*
Clifford, Ebenezer, 90
Codman, John, 44, 47, 52, 99, 123
Codman, Ogden, Jr., 52, 98, 101, 123, *123,* 183
Codman, Ogden, Sr., and Sarah, family, 52, *52,* 99, 101, 102, 106, 120, 123, *123,* 124, 131, 147, 163, 183

Codman House (The Grange), 14, *22, 25, 34,* 44, *44–45,* 52, *53, 57, 98, 99, 99, 100–101, 101,* 106, *106,* 122, 123, *123,* 128–29, 147, 148, *171,* 183, *199*
Coffin, Tristram, Jr., and Judith, family, 81, 82, 83, 85, 102, 109, 124, 132, 159, 179, *179*
Coffin House, *36, 80–81,* 81, *82, 82–83, 83,* 85, 89, 102, *108–9,* 109, 132, *132–33,* 138, *139,* 141, 142, *143,* 156, *158–59, 178–79,* 179, *199*
Cogswell, Jonathan, family, 66, 67
Cogswell, William, 189
Cogswell (William) House, *189*
Cogswell's Grant, 40, *41,* 66, *66,* 67, *177,* 189, 194, *194, 195, 199*
Cook, Eliza, 31
Cooper-Frost-Austin House, 14, *200*
Copley, John Singleton, 182
The Country Builder's Assistant (Benjamin), 72
Winslow Crocker House, *192–93, 193, 200*
Cummings, Abbott Lowell, 135, 197
Currier and Ives, 185

Codman House (The Grange), 14, *22,*
Dearing, Ebenezer, 68
The Decoration of Houses (Wharton and Codman), 101
Deephaven (Jewett), 26, 35, 167, 194
Diderot, Denis, 10
Dole-Little House, *200*
Downing, Andrew Jackson, 51, 76, 96
Dudley, William Perry, 14, 190
du Pont, Henry Francis, 135
Dyer, Henry A., 51

Eliot, Charles W., 10
Emerson, Ralph Waldo, 22
Emmet, Alan, 39
Encyclopédie (Diderot), 10

Fernald, George Porter, 54, 186
Fields, Annie, 128
Fisher, Alvan, 47
Foster, William, 93
Fowler House, 14
Franklin, Benjamin, 9, 10, 190, *191*

Gardner, Isabella Stewart, *171,* 189, *189*
Gay, Ernest, 14
Gedney House, *200*
Gilman, John, 14
Gilman Garrison House, *12–13, 64–65,* 190, *190,* 200
Godey's Lady's Book, 31

Goodwin family, 54, 106
Gore, Christopher and Rebecca, 18, 44, 161
Gore, John, 180
Gore Place, 18, 44
Gould family, 43
Grant, Ulysses S., 120
Gropius, Ise and Walter, 15, 57, 59, 60, 79, 152, 172, 197
Gropius House, 15, 29, 31, *56–57,* 57, *58–59,* 60, *60–61, 102, 152–53, 153, 172, 173,* 200

Haggins, John, 68
Hamilton, Jonathan, 54, 185
Hamilton House, *1, 20, 21,* 25, 35, 54, *54–55,* 102, 106, *106–7,* 131, *131,* 167, *184,* 185, *185, 186–87,* 189, 197, *201*
Hampton Court, England, 47, 167
Hancock, Thomas, 12
John Hancock House, 12, 14
Harrison, Benjamin, *164*
Sally Hart House, 186
Hawthorne, Nathaniel, opposite 1, 32
Holmes, Oliver Wendell, 10
House and Garden (magazine), 59

House Beautiful (magazine), 189
The House of the Seven Gables (Hawthorne), opposite 1
The House Servant's Directory (Roberts), 161, 163
Huse family, 132, 138

Indian Hill, 189
Irving and Casson, 79

Jackson House, *62, 148, 201*
Jefferson, Thomas, 74, 95
Jewett, Sarah Orne, 26, 35, 54, 68, 102, 124, 128, 131, 167, *174–75*, 180, 182, *185*, 194, 197
Sarah Orne Jewett House, 89, *89, 102–3, 166, 174–75, 201*
Johnson, Samuel, 10

Keller, Helen, *124*

Lafayette, Marquis de, 190, *191*
Langdon, John and Elizabeth, family, 68, 78, 79, 89, 90, *90*, 96, 102, 113, 124
Governor John Langdon House, *7, 23*, 68, *68, 69, 78*, 78–79, *79*, 90, *90, 90–91, 112–13, 113*, 124, *201*

Little, Amelia and Agnes, 168, 197
Little, Bertram K. and Nina Fletcher, 176, 194, 197
Longfellow, Alice, 14
Longfellow, Henry Wadsworth, 29
Lowell, James Russell, 9, 10
Lyman, Arthur and Ella, family, 105, 106, *106*, 120, 167, 183
Lyman, Theodore, 47, 162
Lyman Estate (The Vale), *7, 11, 25, 32, 46, 47, 47*, 106, 167, 183, *183, 201*
Lyman House (Boston), *104–5, 120*

MacLeish, Archibald, 25
Marcotte, Leon, 99, 101
Marrett, Daniel, family, 48, 75, 76, 124, 132, 142, 167, *167*
Marrett House, *7, 32, 74, 75, 124*, 131, 142, *143, 144–45, 145, 201*
Massachusetts Society for Promoting Agriculture (MSPA), 44, 47, May, James Rundlet, family, 124, 183

McCall's (magazine), 172, *172*
McCann, Helena Woolworth, family, 190
McCord, David, 11
McIntire, Samuel, 47
McKim, Mead, and White, 78–79
Merwin House, *147, 202*
Mills, Richard, 68

Nickels, William, 72
Nickels-Sortwell House, *2–3*, 72, *72, 73, 172, 172, 202*

Otis, Harrison Gray and Sally, family, 71, 89, 93, 96, 102, 114, 162, 163
Harrison Gray Otis House, *32, 70–71, 71, 72, 92–93*, 93, 114, *115, 162, 162–63, 163*, 197, *202*

Pain, William, 67, 72
Parloa, Maria, 168
Peirce, Daniel, Jr., 64
Phillips, Wendell, 10
Pierce, Edward, 67
Pierce House, *202*
The Practical House Carpenter (Pain), 72

Quincy, Josiah, Sr., family, 67, 89, 159, 182, *182*
Quincy House, *6, 67, 67, 88–89*, 89, 159, 182, *182–83, 202*

Paul Revere Association, 14
Paul Revere House, 14
Reynolds, Jonathan Phillips, Jr., 14
Roberts, Robert, 161, 163
Rocky Hill Meeting House, *29, 37, 202*
Rumford, Count, 135, 136, 141
Rundlet, James and Jane, family, 48, 89, 95, 96, 102, 117, 120, 136, 161, 163
Rundlet-May House, 48, *49, 94–95*, 95, *116–17*, 117, 124, *124–25*, 136, *136*, 141, 142, *143*, 148, *148–49*, 151, *160–61*, 161, 183, *203*

Savage, Edward, 90
Sayward, Jonathan, family, *84, 85, 86*, 89, 102, 110, *110*, 113, 126, 132, 156, 180, *180*. *See also* Barrell, Elizabeth and Mary; Wheeler, Elizabeth Cheever
Sayward-Wheeler House, 15, *84, 85, 85*, 86, *86–87*, 110, *110–11*, 126, *126–27*, 131, 156, *156–57*, 180, *180–81*, 197, *203*
Sewall, Samuel, 85

A Sketch of the History of Newbury, Newburyport, and West Newbury (Coffin), 179
Sleeper, Henry Davis, 17, 135, 171, *171*, 189, *189*, 190, 193
Smith, Adam, 10
Society for the Preservation of New England Antiquities (SPNEA), 10, 11, 14, 15, 17, 40, 44, 52, 57, 63, 71, 168, 179, 190, 194, 196, 197
Sortwell family, 172, *172*
Spencer-Peirce-Little Farm, *18–19*, 40, *40*, 117, 142, *152*, 168, *203*
Spencer-Peirce-Little House, *endleaves, 64, 64*, 156, *168–69*, 196
Spring, James W., 81
Storer, Bellamy and Maria, *171*
Sturgis, John Hubbard, 98, 99
Swan, Abraham, 67, 68
Swett-Ilsley House, 14, *203*

Thacher, Mary, family, 193, *193*
Thompson, Benjamin. *See* Count Rumford
Thoreau, Henry David, 21, 36,

Tracy, Nathaniel, family, 156, 159
A Treatise on Domestic Economy (Beecher), 163
A Treatise on the Theory and Practice of Landscape Gardening (Downing), 51
Tucker, Richard, Jr., and Mollie, family, 96, 118, *118*, 124, 136, 138, 141, 147, 156, 164, 168
Tyson, Emily and Elise, 54, 102, 167, 185, *185, 186*, 189, 197

Walpole, Horace, 190
Washington, George, 113
Watson Farm, *4–5, 6, 24*, 40, *203*
The Wealth of Nations (Smith), 10
Wells, Joseph Collins, 76, 145
Wharton, Edith, 101
Wheeler, Elizabeth Cheever, family, 126
Whidden, Michael, 68
Whitefield, Edwin, 82
Whitman, Sarah Wyman, 102
Whitman, Walt, 10
Winterthur Museum, 135
Woodbury, Marcia Oakes, 167

First edition

Library of Congress Cataloging-in-Publication Data
Nylander, Jane C.
    Windows on the past : four centuries of New England homes / Jane C. Nylander with Diane Viera ; Society for the Preservation of New England Antiquities ; color photographs by David Bohl ; foreword by Wendell Garrett — 1st ed.
        p. cm.
    ISBN 0-8212-2483-2 (hardcover)
    1. Historical museums—New England. 2. Historic buildings—New England. 3. Dwellings—New England—History. 4. New England—Social life and customs. 5. New England—Antiquities—Collection and preservation. 6. Historical museums—New England—Pictorial works. 7. Historic buildings—New England—Pictorial works. 8. Dwellings—New England—Pictorial works. I. Viera, Diane. II. Society for the Preservation of New England Antiquities. III. Title.
    F5 N95 2000
    974—dc21   99-049516

Bulfinch Press is an imprint and trademark of Little, Brown and Company Inc.

Produced by Archetype Press, Inc., Washington, D.C.; Diane Maddex, Project Director; Gretchen Smith Mui, Editor; Carol Kim, Editorial Assistant; Robert L. Wiser, Designer

Printed in Hong Kong

Grateful acknowledgment is also made for use of the following photographs and quotations. *Photographs:* Page 68, bottom left: Courtesy Boston Athenaeum. Page 171, bottom, and page 189, top: Courtesy A. Piatt Andrew Archive. Pages 174–75: Courtesy Houghton Library, Harvard University. *Quotations:* Page 25: From "Immortal Autumn," *Collected Poems 1917–1982* by Archibald MacLeish; copyright © 1985 by The Estate of Archibald MacLeish; reprinted by permission of Houghton Mifflin Company; all rights reserved. Page 67: Courtesy Massachusetts Historical Society. Pages 110 and 113 (Sayward diary quotations): Courtesy American Antiquarian Society. Page 113 (Langdon furnishings and contract quotations): Courtesy Strawbery Banke. Page 114: Courtesy Massachusetts Historical Society.

Case binding: "Green Worm," an English wallpaper installed in 1809 in the Rundlet-May House. End-leaves: Graffiti in the attic of the Spencer-Peirce-Little House. Page 1: The Hamilton House and its garden in winter. Pages 2–3: The Nickels-Sortwell House. Pages 4–5: Some of the flock at the Watson Farm. Pages 6–7: (top, left to right) the Watson Farm, the greenhouse at the Lyman Estate, and the Barrett House; (bottom, left to right) the Quincy House, the Governor John Langdon House, and the Marrett House.